COUNTING THE YEARS

REAL-LIFE STORIES ABOUT WAITING FOR LOVED ONES TO RETURN HOME FROM PRISON

The Think Outside the Cell Series
Edited by Sheila R. Rule and Marsha R. Rule

RESILIENCE
MULTIMEDIA

For information about this title or to order other books and/or electronic media, contact the publisher:

Resilience Multimedia
511 Avenue of the Americas, Suite 525
New York, NY 10011
www.thinkoutsidethecell.org
877-267-2303

ISBN: 978-0-9791599-2-3
Printed in the United States of America
Cover and interior design: 1106 Design

Please note: The image used on the cover is being used for illustrative purposes only. The woman depicted is a model. (Photo: iStockPhoto.com)

*For the children
of the incarcerated*

Contents

ACKNOWLEDGEMENTS

First, I am deeply grateful to all of the contributors for their talent, courage, and honesty in telling the real stories of their lives.

I am deeply grateful, too, to the Ford Foundation, without whose generous support this book and others in *The Think Outside the Cell Series* would not have been possible. I am particularly thankful for the kind heart and creative vision of one of the foundation's program officers, Calvin Sims.

Special praise to members of my family, whose love for me has always been a powerful action verb: my mother, Versa Rule; my sisters, Marsha and Diana; my nieces, Michaela and Alana; and, of course, my son, Sean.

For her sharp editing skills and enthusiastic embrace of this project, my heartfelt thanks to Kathleen McElroy.

Finally, I thank Joe, who is more than worth the wait.
—*Sheila R. Rule*

I am deeply grateful to Sheila Rule and Joseph Robinson for their tremendous vision of creating a venue where the voices of the incarcerated and formerly incarcerated can be heard, again and again and again.

I want to thank the authors of this collection for the gift of their stories and for reminding me of the interconnectedness of all of our lives.

And, of course, my great appreciation to all the wonderful relationships in my life!
—*Marsha R. Rule*

INTRODUCTION

More than 2.3 million people are incarcerated in the United States. Millions upon millions of others—among them wives and husbands, mothers and fathers, sisters and brothers, daughters and sons—wait for their return.

Some wait quietly. They go about the daily routines of living. They welcome the collect phone calls from their locked-away loved ones, and travel whatever the distance to pay them regular visits. They cry. They pray. They live in hope.

Others make some noise while they wait. They put muscle to their longing. They organize. They lobby their legislators. With posters held high, they demonstrate for changes in laws, changes in policies, changes in anything that will result in their loved ones coming home.

Many wait and struggle—to put food on the table, to pay for those costly collect calls, to protect their families from being swallowed whole by poverty. With the incarceration of a family member who may have been the main source of financial support, the struggle to make ends meet looms ever larger and threatens to overshadow everything else. And in a world where monitored letters, monitored phone calls, and monitored visits pass for normal, they struggle to maintain family ties and some degree of intimacy.

There are also those who wait until the waiting becomes too great. They grow tired. They give up. They leave.

Counting the Years: Real-Life Stories about Waiting for Loved Ones to Return Home from Prison illuminates the weight of the wait experienced by families and friends of the incarcerated. This anthology allows them to share their longing and their lives. The hope is that, over time, hearing these stories and others like them will lead the larger society to put aside stereotypes and myths about this population and see them for who they really are; they are like the rest of us. And in telling their stories, the people of this largely forgotten population might inspire, encourage, and motivate those in similar situations.

The idea for this book had its roots in volunteer work that I began nearly a decade ago, after joining the Prison Ministry of the Riverside Church, a New York church internationally recognized for its commitment to social justice. I was asked to correspond with incarcerated men and women who wrote to the organization. And so I did.

Although generally dehumanized and demonized, the people I came to know through letters were multidimensional, complex human beings. More than a few were skilled and talented in a range of disciplines, from art and music to sociology, business, and the law. And many had used their time in prison to rethink and disavow the values and belief systems that had brought them there.

The people I came to know were much greater than the bad choices they'd made. And they so inspired me that I would eventually found and devote myself to a publishing company that, as part of its mission, would seek to present a more balanced view of the incarcerated through books that would allow them a voice and help them tackle some of the hard challenges they face.

My husband, Joseph Robinson—for whom I wait, and make some noise while doing so—helped to give definition and structure to my book idea. He suggested that I develop a series of books that portray the realities, gifts, and diversity of experiences of people with prison in their backgrounds. The series would take its name from the title of the book he wrote several years ago to help people currently or formerly in prison to use their innate gifts to build successful lives: *Think Outside the Cell: An Entrepreneur's Guide for the Incarcerated and Formerly Incarcerated.* Other books in the Think Outside the Cell Series include *Love Lives Here, Too: Real-Life Stories about Prison Marriages and Relationships,* and *The Hard Journey Home: Real-Life Stories about Reentering Society after Incarceration.*

Contributors to *Counting the Years* write about waiting from various standpoints. For Lowanna Owens, waiting for her son to return home from prison was something she could never have contemplated: "We were a 'Bill Cosby' family, educated blacks with class and standards. We were middle class, lived in the suburbs outside of Los Angeles, and had a loving extended family. All was good. Or so I thought. Of our three children, Preston is our middle child...He could run fast, his eye-hand coordination was impressive, and he was good in all sports...He had excellent manners...There was childhood mischief, but we never considered that a sign of future problems. He was all boy, with the promise of being a great athlete with good looks and intelligence."

Franklin Ray Brown's children thought that an initiative on an election ballot would be his ticket home: "Before the election, polls had the initiative to repeal the law winning. For my family that meant that within ninety days after its approval, my children would have their dad home...The joy and excitement that I heard in their voices made me feel that I would be able to be a real father for the first time. We counted the days until the election."

Delores Mariano recalls the end of her wait for her incarcerated daughter: "I sit and stare at that gate and those fences that have held her all these months. I wonder how she will be when she walks through the gate. Will there be the hateful yelling, and the pushing away of the baby she can't deal with? Or will she have truly changed? Will she be able to demonstrate heartfelt love and acceptance of her child? Will she learn to care for and love the child who looks at her pictures and calls out 'Mama?' I wonder...Here she comes. My heart races; I am actually scared to death. I don't want her to come through that gate."

Ashley White shares the ordeal surrounding her weekly visits to her husband: "At this point, I'm beat. I got up at 1:00 a.m. I left my house at 2:00 a.m. I'm just about to shut my eyes when I see his face coming through the heavy metal door that slams behind him. He looks at me and smiles. I'm happy to see him but sick of all this crap I have to go through to get in here to see him for six hours a week. We sit next to each other, hold hands, and briefly kiss. All we can do is talk and fantasize about when he comes home…It's so loud…I can't concentrate. I start fights with my husband because I just can't act 'normal' in here. I laugh, and then I cry."

Ebonny Fowler recalls how, days before her fourteenth birthday, she waited for her brother to come home with a gift of sneakers: "Jamal never made it home that night. He was wrongfully arrested for a crime he didn't commit and has spent the last twenty years in prison. I've been waiting for my brother to come back home for two decades—240 months; 7,306 days, and counting…For the last twenty years I've been constantly waiting…Waiting for my brother to be exonerated."

And Jeff Smith shares how his wait ended in the greatest tragedy for any parent: "Since Saturday I have been speaking of my son, Whitney, in the past tense. I would, of course, rather take my own life than to acknowledge so actively the reality of what has happened with my own speaking voice, and it would be a far easier thing. But today is the day which has been chosen to honor his life, since that is now the only thing left to us to do for him."

I hope that *Counting the Years* honors all those who wait, and that the stories here help to illuminate how the impact of our nation's little-debated criminal justice policies reaches far beyond prison walls.

> *—Sheila R. Rule*
> *Publisher*
> *Resilience Multimedia*
> *September 2010*

Jeff Smith

The Greatest Tragedy

My son, Whitney Smith, had served just over three years of his six-year sentence at the United States Penitentiary in Terre Haute, Indiana, when he died of an apparent suicide. Although he was allowed to receive all-day visits from me once a month and we spoke every few days on the phone, it was chiefly through letters that we maintained and even strengthened the bond that had always existed between us—especially during the last fifteen months of his life, when he was placed in solitary confinement with no visiting or phone privileges.

During those three years, we wrote several letters a week to each other, covering every subject imaginable: politics, science, philosophy, sports; the travails, dangers, and injustices of prison life; his evolving plans for his future after prison. Whit himself noted early on that as awful as the circumstances were, the act of letter writing was bringing us even closer together than we might have become otherwise, and he wanted me to know how grateful he was for that. Had he survived prison, we would have enjoyed the fruits of that relationship deepening for the rest of our lives. As it is, the survivor is left with the bittersweet recognition of what we had offset against what could have been.

Among many other things, the life of an inmate is about waiting: for the next letter—at least if you're fortunate enough to have someone who writes to you—and ultimately for the day you're finally released. But for the countless loved ones and families of the incarcerated—myself included—life becomes almost defined by the wait, as well. It becomes the act of holding your breath for years at a time, the sense that life will remain incomplete until your loved one comes home. In my case, it wasn't about passively waiting out the time. I saw my role as not only providing support as a lifeline to home and family, but also as an active participant in Whit's personal journey. And our relationship was such that he *invited* me to participate, sharing with me his honest, innermost fears, joys, sorrows, hopes, and plans for the future, and always asking for advice. There was a tacit understanding that we needed each other.

I knew Whit was coming home, and I knew that if he were to realize all of his beautiful potential after returning, he would need continuous encouragement along the way. I'm sure my own friends and family thought that my devotion sometimes bordered on the excessive—since phone calls from inmates weren't allowed to cell phone numbers, I had call forwarding permanently set on my landline so that no matter where I was, I would never miss a call. Oddly enough, relating to Whit was not unlike what many parents experience in "normal" circumstances. Assuming you're fortunate enough to have a child who actually does ask for and appreciate help, he or she will still sometimes point out when you're smothering or giving too much. Like any other young person, Whit needed enough freedom to find his own way. To his everlasting credit—and as an indication of how strong our relationship was—Whit was honest and forthright enough to lovingly tell me when I needed to back off, even as he would be quick to assure me that even that particular heavy-handed intervention was appreciated. Unconditional love was a given, but mutual trust was the bottom line of our relationship.

As hard as these years were for me as a parent, I knew full well how much more Whit suffered, and how hard he worked to earn both his own self-respect and the devotion of those who loved him. This was perhaps best put at his memorial service by Michael Millard, a close friend of mine from Vermont who met Whit in person for the first and last time at Terre Haute in 2007:

"When I met Whit, he had really begun to ask himself (as a grown man), 'So, what IS it with me?' He saw the trail behind and asked, 'Why?' He did NOT understand. He asked these things fully and honestly. There was no 'right answer;' he wanted the truth. And he did most of the work of understanding the why and wherefore of his life, which most of us do between the ages of twenty-five and fifty years, in the four years from twenty to twenty-five. He began, in all facets of his life, to take full responsibility for himself, his choices, and his actions.

If you need any measure of the quality of the man, I ask you to envision a twenty-year-old learning this in the context of the hell which is Terre Haute F.C.C. This is an extraordinary human being."

So that's what I was waiting for. To see that extraordinary human being who was my son come home and flourish in the world.

Instead, I found myself in the unfathomably desperate situation of having to write these words to read at his memorial:

"A short time ago I was part, without taking part, of a memorial for a young girl who was taken from her parents and family. It hurt me to the core, and still does. I now know part of the reason why that is so. It's not only that I have always been constitutionally unable to keep from going straight to the hurt of others and absorbing it. It's also because I have always known the loss of my son or daughter would be the greatest tragedy of my life. And here I am.

Since Saturday I have been speaking of my son, Whitney, in the past tense. I would, of course, rather take my own life than to acknowledge so actively the reality of what has happened with my own speaking voice, and it would be a far easier thing. But today is the day which has been chosen to honor his life, since that is now the only thing left to us to do for him.

There are often remembrances that provoke kind, poignant laughter at a memorial. I will not be the one who is able to provide that, but I know, and am grateful, that others will.

Whit's life was painfully short, and it was painful and short. But it was only the last half that was so full of pain. Whit was a curious, fun-loving, sensitive, and kind boy. There is scarcely one of you here who knew him personally, and perhaps even some who did not, who was not at one time or another the recipient of a random act of kindness from Whit. This began in his earliest life, when he bestowed these unexpectedly and in various forms on his parents. Cards, notes, even a card I found recently with fifteen cents taped inside, given I suppose when he was seven or eight. He loved to surprise with expressions of love and gratitude.

He loved animals, and was devastated when he had to see our first dog struck and killed by a car when he was quite young. He and his grandfather fashioned a cement grave marker with a big heart fingered into the unset concrete. I still have a mouse pad made from a photo of him sitting happily on a chair, holding the next dog, his beloved Milli Vanilli.

I cannot begin to tell of all the ways, large and small, in which his generous, caring, and, yes, in some way fragile, spirit shone through. His life was a crooked path. It can be said, depending on your views about these things, that he made bad choices, and that they were his to make. Or that he was compelled to make them as part of his nature, no less than the beautiful, non-self-defeating side. First of all, I tend to see those choices as an aspect of his inherent creativity. That he did things that were considered hurtful to his family, and later ones violated the norms of society, all came, I believe, as a surprise to him. Not that they were hurtful, but that, in retrospect, he had done them. He was never able to understand why, as hard as he

11

tried. And it was not because he didn't try. He was exquisitely thoughtful and self-aware. And part of what always hurt me was to see how helpless he felt from that inability to understand it himself. There were some who considered his self-defeating actions, even the extreme ones, as nothing more than willful self-indulgence. I always knew better.

I was always the one who gave him the benefit of the doubt. It was not that I couldn't or didn't see the consequences his actions had on others, and that they were hurtful to him, as well. But as for his early life, you only need to listen to the others who will speak in both his and their own voices, to understand what it was I saw.

His continual, honest search for identity at some point brought him to prison, once and then again. Rather than be discouraged by the actions that brought him there, I somehow was always able to see even that in the context of a whole life, knowing with absolute certainty who he was in his core, and what he had the potential to become. Every single word in the thousands of letters he wrote to me, from Dayton and then Terre Haute, was painfully honest, insightful, and indisputably genuine evidence of and justification for my faith in him.

Today a comment was posted on his blog, from someone who didn't leave a name, which reads: '*I came across this blog today while doing research for my job. I have been reading these posts and they have brought laughter and sorrow. Your son was brilliant, creative, and intelligent. I only wish that I had found these writings sooner. My heart is with your family.*'

Which brings me to Whitney's blog. Last November he told me he wanted to write one, and asked if I would set it up for him. Since he had no access to a computer, he wrote each entry by hand and mailed it to me. It didn't become an overnight success, but it has grown to hundreds of regular readers from all over the world. And the numbers have grown exponentially since Saturday. It will remain the most publicly visible and successful manifestation of and testament to his beauty, honesty, and depth of soul.

I have to say in this context that I am personally ambivalent about the meaningfulness and significance of memorial services like this. I find it too easy to try and reject reality as not real and not true, and find only abject irony in being forced into this situation, as if remembering my son could do anything for *him* now. Which is ultimately the only thing that matters to me, even now. But at the same time, for whatever reasons, whether of any *ultimate* meaning or not, I am compelled to wish the entire world would read his words and hear his voice. I myself cannot do so without the pain of disconnect, but others can.

I find it tragic that his place and condition dictated that some of his most creative expression had to come from writing about his utter pain, frustration, depression, and the inherently inhumane conditions under which he was forced to live. Yes, of course, that's all he had to write about, and of course it was in part the extremity of his existence that made his writing so powerful—though not only, because he wrote well and beautifully of many things throughout his life. One of his readers described his writing once as "seriously vivid," and while there are many equally apt descriptions, I've always liked this one. And had it been allowed to be just a stage of development, fodder for something to come later, I would feel less angry and cheated—for his sake and all of ours—by the necessity of the subject matter. But that cannot be changed, and we have this permanent record of a beautiful voice calling out from one of the worst places on earth. He uses humor often, even as a basic device; that is because he has a natural sense of humor, and because it is the only way he can get even a little bit of distance from the pain and horror.

The world is not a very nice place. But Whit's very existence was an infinitely beautiful thing for me. And the world is at least nice enough, and Whit's soul such an incomparably beautiful one, that he deserved more life, but he also deserved better than what life gave him. I will believe with absolute certainty, for as long as I have left to live, that had the prison system not broken him, he would have come home a whole person and made the world a *better* place. He was finding his voice, and his true, beautiful self was winning the internal struggle. He was ready to come home. He had plans and ambitions.

I would like to finish now by reading the last thing I wrote to my son. It was a birthday card, and I am not even sure whether he received it. The sentiment on the card reads:

'Your journey has molded you for your greater good, and it was exactly what it needed to be. Don't think that you've lost time. It took each and every situation you have encountered to bring you to the now. And now is right on *time*.'

And inside I wrote:

'I may not be Zen-like enough to buy into the first sentence, or at least the second clause, but I have always tried to embrace it, and it would be well if you're able to. I know; it's hard not to wish there had been a different, less painful path taking you to the same destination. But as for the rest of this view, I'm definitely a subscriber. I know who you've always been, who you are today, and I see who you're becoming, and I could not be more proud. So no, don't think that you've lost time. Look at what you've been able to become and accomplish in such adverse conditions, and then imagine how it will feel to take that and run with it in a world that's wide open to you. Hemingway wrote: "The world breaks everyone, and afterwards some are stronger in the broken places." That's you.

So as you turn twenty-five, don't dwell on the past but take what you need from it to carry with you into the future. Some of it comes in the form of a burden, but never forget how many people are walking beside you, eager to help you carry that part until it can be put down and left behind.'

I was always proud of my son. There was never a moment when I lost faith in him. I hope every one of you comes away from this understanding why he deserved that."

Whitney Holwadel Smith

An Oral History of My Future

Not long ago I finished reading "The Story of Joe Gould." The Story of Joe Gould as told by Joseph Mitchell, a columnist and staff writer at *The New Yorker* magazine from the 1930s until the mid-60s.

Mr. Joe Gould was quite the enigma. Sometimes monikered "Professor," sometimes "Professor Sea Gull" due to his self-professed mastering of the mightily elusive seagull language.

Born a true Yankee just outside of Boston in 1889, the inadequate son to a successful physician father, Gould constantly felt like an outcast at home, so after graduation from Harvard he left Massachusetts for New York City, where he ultimately settled into the life of a bohemian. Of course this was back when Bohemianism could be loosely considered a profession.

Living solely off his friends' contributions to "The Joe Gould Fund," Gould spent his days an eccentric, drinking and interacting with the city's pop society of the time, inviting himself to parties or shocking people with his poetry readings, some of which had been translated into seagull.

But the main focus of his life was a book he was writing called "An Oral History of Our Time," which was said at the time to be the longest unpublished work in existence. Over the years Gould could consistently be found scribbling away in his grammar school composition books, which were invariably greasy and coffee-stained from his "rugged" lifestyle. He would carry a few with him at all times, while others were stashed in the closets of various friends' apartments. But the bulk of the material was said to be stored in a farmhouse cellar in upstate New York. This stockpile allegedly contained a stack of notebooks seven feet high. Containing first six, then seven, then eight, then nine million words.

The Oral History was Joe Gould's meal ticket. It was a collection of random essays and commentary on conversations overheard or participated in by Gould and thought by him to be indicative of the state of our country at the period of the Second World War; a piece of literature rivaling Gibbon's "The History of the Decline and Fall of the Roman Empire." In reality, several publishers who had read samples from the hundreds of nickel composition books described Gould's writing as "grotesque" or "childish" or simply "illegible." But Gould himself was thoroughly convinced that in posterity his Oral History, the collection of eavesdropped conversations between diner patrons, ambulance drivers, Bellevue asylum interns, and Greenwich Village poets, would be regarded as the principal textbook of American culture. He often proclaimed that his will bequeathed one-third of the Oral History to the Smithsonian Institution and the other two-thirds to the Harvard Library. To be measured by weight.

And Joe wasn't the only one with faith in his tome. There were dozens of men and women who supported his long career as a bohemian and who all (or most) had faith that this epic piece of writing would more than justify the years of weekly contributions to the Joe Gould Fund.

So upon news of his death in a mental institution in 1957 at the age of sixty-eight, there was a mad scramble among his friends and acquaintances to find these composition books. But where were they? Apart from the ten or so scattered among a few artists' closets, nobody had any idea where the actual collection "a dozen times longer than the Bible" was. It was common knowledge that they were supposed to be hidden away in the farmhouse basement, but Gould had always been vague and cryptic when answering any questions about the location of this farmhouse or the name of its owner. The stash was never found, and never will be. The Oral History does not exist. For lack of a better word, the Oral History was a scam.

Joseph Mitchell had done a lengthy profile of Joe Gould for *The New Yorker;* this is the piece I just finished reading in an anthology of Mitchell's contributions to the magazine. Even after the profile was completed and printed, their relationship continued for years. During that period Mitchell had opportunity to read quite a few chapters of the Oral History, except that he found each was only one of five different chapters, all rewrites of each other; different formats but clearly the same topics. A sculptor friend of Gould who often stored some of the notebooks told Mitchell that in all the years he had been keeping the chapters, they had all been on the same subjects, only hundreds of different drafts.

It was this oddity and an incident with a publisher Mitchell had tried to set Gould up with that provoked the outburst which consequently revealed that the nine million words simply did not exist. The upstate New York farmhouse was a lie. The Oral History of Our Time was nothing more than a delusion of grandeur.

Not wanting to break the spirit of an old man whose almost entire existence revolved around a myth, Mitchell kept Gould's secret until well after the latter's death, even assisting in the grand wild goose chase for the missing notebooks.

Joe Gould spent decades of his life preaching to anyone who would listen that he was the author of an epic work of historical literature which never existed. It's anyone's guess why he never got past those initial five chapters. He may have intended his whole life to eventually get around to writing down the conversation he quoted from memory. But at some point he surely convinced even himself that somewhere there really was a cellar with two meters of stained and dog-eared notebooks stored there. And real or not, the Oral History as a concept sustained him.

In just a few months I will be "celebrating" the milestone of having spent seven of my twenty-four years as a prisoner. For seven years I have done my best to convince whomever will listen that the future of Whitney Holwadel Smith is a bet worth wagering. I've prophesied the college degrees, the good jobs, the on-time mortgage payments, and tax refunds. In my rhetoric to family and friends who have all in their own way contributed to the "Whitney Smith Fund," I present a character in a vaguely written play who is unremarkable as a citizen and remarkable as a concept of myself, the two-time felon.

With more than half of my current sentence done and a little over three years to go, I should be giddy about the prospect of proving my words to be more than just empty rhetoric. But the mundane nature of my life in the hole has all but deadened my hope and anticipation. I have begun to wonder if all those things I claimed to my "contributors" are real or just a series of fictions which I have even convinced myself of.

I am teetering on the edge of becoming institutionalized.

After spending three years in a medium-security Ohio prison, a friend of mine once asked me if the time spent there had institutionalized me. At the time my idea of what it meant to be institutionalized consisted of simply forming habits specific to life in prison. So I answered that yes, I had become institutionalized to a certain extent.

But I was wrong. It is impossible to truly know what it is to be institutionalized without actually experiencing it. To be institutionalized means to adapt your mind completely to life enclosed by walls and razor wire. It is the transformation of the outside world from a real place and a goal to simply a novelty; a queer thing that's written about in the newspapers but with about as much significance as Los Angeles has to a poor Ethiopian villager. Institutionalization occurs somewhere around the time when a prisoner says, "I can't wait to get home" and is referring to his cell.

I've spent seven years trying to convince those I care about that I am worthy of their contributions. But are they empty promises? Will the time come to pass that, like Gould's five raggedy installments, I cannot see past the chapters of my life spent in a cage? Will this be the only world I truly know? As my mind becomes slowly wrapped in the wet blanket of institutionalization, I am fearing so.

But my promises and hope are all I have left; I cannot abandon them.

These are the thoughts which consume a prisoner on a daily basis. This prisoner, at least.

—Whitney Holwadel Smith
Born April 10, 1984
Died April 4, 2009

This piece appeared on Whitney's blog of December 15, 2008.

Lowanna M. Owens

Our Favorite Son

W e were a "Bill Cosby" family, educated blacks with
class and standards. We were middle class, lived in
the suburbs outside of Los Angeles, and had a loving extended
family. All was good. Or so I thought.

Of our three children, Preston is our middle child. He
received lots of attention for being so cute, for his curly hair,
for his charming personality. He was a bubbly and happy child.
He was loving and protective of both his sisters. He made
friends easily and was popular with girls. He could run fast,
his eye-hand coordination was impressive, and he was good in
all sports, especially soccer and basketball. He had excellent
manners. He was disciplined and did his chores. There was
childhood mischief, but we never considered that a sign of

future problems. He was all boy, with the promise of being a great athlete with good looks and intelligence.

Until inner-city black boys started moving into our city and going to our schools, our son didn't know that some blacks acted differently from him. Why did he follow them when so many other young black men who grew up with him did not? He started getting into trouble. I kept waiting for him to change, to grow up, to mature, to "learn his lesson." I tried to organize a parents' group at his high school, but the school did not want to admit there was a problem. The problems grew.

The young men from the inner city who were new to the neighborhood were street smart; our son was not. He did time; they did not. Our son graduated from high school in 1998 and went to prison in 2000.

My husband and I made our first visit to California State Prison-Corcoran on a Saturday that year. When we arrived, we were turned away. Visiting hours were over. I couldn't stop crying.

We spent the night in Bakersfield and returned to the prison the following day, only to be told my clothing was not on the prison's approved list—wrong color. I had to go to the visitors' center to find acceptable clothing. That process affected my identity, as I knew it in "my world."

On the third visit, Corcoran was on lockdown. That affected our sense of having any connection to our son's safety. On our fourth visit, our son had been moved from a minimum-level section to a higher-level section. Not knowing what had happened or why confirmed for us that he was on his own, and that neither he nor the prison staff would tell us if he was safe or where he was. Our son would try to protect us from worry or the truth; the prison staff would protect themselves from accountability or publicity.

For three years, we visited faithfully once a month. When we weren't waiting to see him on visiting days, we were waiting to get his phone call. We waited in line at Wal-Mart to pay for his prison-approved purchases, waited at the post office to mail him a box, waited to get money orders for his books. We waited for the mail carrier to deliver his letters, and we waited for time to pass on his sentence.

In spite of the strain on our marriage and our family, waiting for our son to return from prison made us fiercely protective. And we grew closer. Long-time friendships were affected— some grew closer, others more distant. The emotional strain on our other two children—one in college and the other in high school—proved that their character was strong.

Our finances never recuperated; we refinanced and borrowed trying to save our son. While waiting, I made a tab of the dollar amounts spent to save our son. Maybe one day he can pay us back, if not with money, in his success as a man. I spent too much money on clothes and accessories, trying to look "sharp as a tack" to camouflage my low self-esteem fueled by thoughts that society had labeled us parental failures.

While waiting, we continued to work, avoiding the stares, whispers, and questions. At both our jobs there were members of our community who knew our sad story. Most were supportive. But as active community members since 1978, we faced the daily burden of trying to overcome the stigma of our son, who was raised in a mainly white and Asian community, becoming a black male statistic.

While waiting, we tried to determine if our parenting would be considered enabling. We decided no—all three of our children were given love, protection, discipline, expectations, and boundaries. And for all three, an example was set for responsibility, hard work, family love, spirituality, education, giving back, and manners.

While waiting, I became obsessed with TV prison shows, newspaper articles about prison, books on criminal behavior, prison web sites, books on young artists with whom our son identified and who had prison experience, like Tupac. When our son was a young teenager, I took away his "gangsta rap" music, and I remember his anger at me for tossing out his Tupac, Snoop Dog, and Little Kim CDs. He now looks at his childhood photos and says I dressed him like a "punk."

While waiting, you blame, you cry, you ask why, you replay over and over in your mind when, where, and how did it all go wrong. There is family anger, as well as personal anger. There is resentment and hostility. It is difficult to communicate because each member of the family is affected so differently.

At first, I lost a lot of weight—no appetite. My husband gained more weight. I eventually became medically obese. Depression came and went. Open and honest communication came and went.

While waiting, I wrote our son obsessively, sometimes twice in the same day. They were letters of encouragement, faith, spirituality, and letters about family happenings. I talked about his being a man, being responsible, being of strong character, and not letting his incarceration keep him from being the best he could be. I wrote poems to him. His dad wrote often, too. I encouraged all who would to write him. A close cousin responded that she didn't know him and didn't know what to say. I would have known what to say to her son had she asked me to do the same. I was terribly hurt by her response. But others who didn't know him did write. And he remembers.

While waiting, I wanted to talk about it and share my pain. My husband wanted to keep it in the family. I went to counseling and left feeling that I was wasting the professional's time. I turned to church and scripture for comfort and peace. Prayer works.

While waiting, our son had my name, "Lowanna," tattooed across his heart in small script—his only tattoo. I don't like tattoos, but maybe that is how he acknowledges me for unconditional love and total honesty in what were probably the worst days of his young life.

While waiting, our older daughter said she lost respect for us as parents, and our younger daughter said she was going to sue us for what she went through. They had no tolerance for their brother making a bad mistake and causing the family such pain. I believe my daughters wanted to give up on their brother. NEVER!

When a child goes to prison and becomes an adult in prison—not necessarily a man, but an adult—family roles and relationships change. And the wait continues after prison to see how that adult will become a man—in spite of himself, in spite of the system, in spite of society—especially when the rules are different for him.

We now wear sadness and disappointment like a permanent cloak. Sadness clouds our optimism. Instead of having enthusiasm for life, we vacillate from distrust to fear to worry to caution—about everything. Emotions remain affected forever. What once was idealism about family life has become a waiting game. That's what happens when life takes a detour down the wrong path.

Our son is home now. When he returned, I was advised to "let it go" and not hold all that has happened against him. I love him dearly, but he is letting society—and himself—hold him back because he is a felon. As long as he lets that happen, I cannot let it go. When he shows us that God and he are in control of what he becomes, then I will let it go. For now, we continue to wait and pray.

Lawrence J. Schulenberg

Everything Has Its Reason

My wife and I delivered our son, Marty, to the Federal Prison Camp in Yankton, South Dakota, on Valentine's Day, 2001.

Thirty-two years earlier, my wife and I drove to Des Moines to pick up our son from the adoption agency, and he came into our family. I was so nervous on that trip, I couldn't drive home. My wife had to drive while I watched the baby in the laundry basket.

That Valentine's Day, our son drove, so his mind would be occupied on something other than the unknown that lay ahead at the end of our trip.

Thinking about that snowy day now brings a lump the size of a boulder to my throat. The movie screen in my mind flashes with pictures of a puppy that used to ride inside Marty's coat; of a little Cub Scout cheering his Pinewood Derby car as he won the race; of a junior handler putting his Miniature Schnauzer through his paces at a dog show until Willie spies us in the stands and races out of the ring; of a high school senior in red cap and gown with tears rolling down his face as I, his principal, bid the class farewell at graduation; of the young man climbing a ladder to replace a burned-out bulb in our garage, as I start the car to begin our trip to Yankton. That's the last thing he would do for us for seven long years.

For weeks and weeks after we delivered Marty to prison, I locked myself in our bathroom, ran the shower full blast, shoved a folded bath towel against my face, and sobbed over what had happened to our family. I cried out to God for His help. I blamed myself for our son's misdeeds.

I wrote letters to our senator in Washington, D.C. I grew up believing that if you "write to your congressman," change would happen. I was positive that as soon as my letter made it to the senator's desk, Marty would be on his way home. Nothing happened. Nothing changed. I joined a number of online prison reform groups. I mailed them my membership fees and received their newsletters. Nothing changed. I wrote "Letters to the Editor." Nothing changed.

I decided that I needed to know what had happened to our son. I wanted to understand addiction. This time, something would change—my attitude and my ignorance.

I enrolled in a substance abuse course at the local community college. I learned that experts do not agree on what causes an addiction, and that knowing the causes isn't as important as dealing with the addiction. I learned about meth, crystal,

crystal meth, ice, fire, croak, speed, crank, glass, crypto, white cross, the damn drug that was responsible for our son being incarcerated three hours away. I became more aware of the tragedy of our son's addiction. And, I came to grips with my feelings of guilt.

When Marty was growing up, we never told him that it was acceptable to break the law. He never witnessed his mother or me relying on alcohol or drugs. He made the choice to use meth that first time. He alone was responsible for the fate that had befallen him.

We loved him more than life itself, and for a long, long time I denied that he was a user. His mother had her suspicions. I knew he was drinking a lot, but I told myself that drinking was a rite of passage for young men. I had drunk more than my share of beer when I was in college, and look, I hadn't ruined my life. He'll be alright, I thought. After all, he had a good job as an auto technician, a girlfriend his mother and I really liked, and friends. Then, the bottom fell out of his world, and ours.

He lost his job. The druggies to whom he owed money took his tools away. His all-terrain vehicle was stolen. His girlfriend told us what was happening and that she was "kicking him out." When we confronted him, the situation got even uglier. His sister accused him of "killing kids." He denied that the drugs he was selling went to young people.

We had been in denial and now we realized Marty, too, was refusing to face the truth. It was only a matter of time. We gave him money to make the "bad guys" go away, but they didn't. We pleaded with him to get help, but he didn't.

We offered to let him come home to live, but he didn't. Our precious son, our little boy, was living on the streets. Every time we heard a siren, we prayed that he wasn't in the back of the ambulance. Every time we saw him, he looked more and more lost. Every time we went to church, we prayed for a rescue.

Finally, after an investigation by the Drug Enforcement Administration, after hiring a lawyer, after visiting him behind glass at a county jail, after going to a court-mandated treatment center, we arrived at that awful moment when we watched our son walk into Yankton Federal Prison Camp, and the door close behind him.

After I fought my way past the feelings of blame and "I did something wrong," after I learned about addiction, after the mail carrier delivered a box containing the clothes Marty had worn to prison, after we had survived that initial visit with him, after my wife and I talked and talked on the return trip home, I vowed that I would do everything possible to make this depressing, stressful, ugly situation of having a child in prison as positive an experience as possible. I wanted to be able to look into my son's eyes and know that he was thankful for my support during this terrible journey. He wouldn't have to say the words, but I would know that I had tried everything to turn this bad time into good time.

Marty's grandfather, now deceased, often said, "Everything has its reason. There is a purpose for everything that happens." My life provided clear examples of that. The polio that I contracted as a small child helped to form the man I have become. The adoptions of our son and daughter made my wife and me better people. The job I hated caused me to find one I loved. I was certain that there was a reason for our son being in prison. If he hadn't gone to prison, we would probably be visiting him in the cemetery. That may be the reason, or it may not. Knowing the reason wasn't as important as making the best of a bad situation. And, that I was determined to do.

I was determined not only for Marty, but also for me. A huge cavern existed in the pit of my stomach. Lara, our daughter, tried to fill that gigantic hole. Not only was she missing her "big brother," she believed that she had to try to "make it all go away" for her mother and me. She called every day to ask how we were doing. While Marty was in prison, Lara was married, received a master's degree, and spent a summer studying at Oxford University, all without her brother, her white knight in shining armor.

Marty's mother worried. She's good at that. She was concerned that he would catch a germ, that he would accidentally not follow a rule and be thrown into the "hole," that he would change from her son into a hardened criminal, that he would not have enough shampoo, that he would hurt himself lifting weights, or take on too much with work and classes. On the road home from visiting our son, Pat would often say, "They've had him long enough. Why can't they just let us take him home?"

As for me, I kept busy. I felt that if I was doing something, if I could push the system, then I was also helping me. So, I sat at my computer and wrote. I cranked out letters to elected officials. I wrote sample letters for members of support groups to use to write their legislators. I became a regular contributor to the "Our Views" column in our local newspaper. I also wrote a book: *To Catch the Snowflakes: A memoir of a polio survivor, a teacher, an adoptive parent, a principal, and the father of an addict.* That was followed by *Willie McGuire and the Land of the People,* a young adult fantasy novel about three children who are patients in the pediatric ward of a hospital. When I finished a chapter, I sent it to the prison camp, where it was read by many of Marty's friends. They begged for more and more pages about "those kids." I dedicated the book to the men of Yankton.

I also accepted an invitation to be a member of the board of directors for the Fourth Judicial District of Iowa, Department of Correctional Services. If I couldn't do anything to help my son, I reasoned, maybe I could do something for the men and women who were incarcerated in our state facilities. And I worked on a grant proposal for Families Also Serve Time (FAST), a program to assist and guide families and friends through the agony of having a loved one in prison.

I wrote to Marty every day. I sent tons of greeting cards to him. I sent copies of all the editorials I had written for those prison reform newsletters. I mailed him bills being considered in Congress. I shared what I was learning at community college. I sent him magazines to occupy his time. I sent him money to buy something a little extra in the commissary. I bought books for his college courses.

We included him in our family's annual Christmas letter and gift exchange. We brought a feast to share at the gathering following his college graduation ceremony.

I never said, "You poor thing." I told him "I love you" every time we spoke on the telephone, and I truly did.

I didn't shy away from the fact that we had a son in prison. I wasn't ashamed of him. I didn't approve of what he had done, but he was still "my boy."

I encouraged our friends and relatives to write to him. Friends, relatives, members of Marty's high school class and their parents kept the post office afloat by all the stamps they bought to send him cards and letters.

We drove to Yankton at least once a month. I figure we spent over 504 hours merely driving to Yankton and back home. We sent at least $16,800 to Yankton. We sat at least 336 hours in the visiting room. We ate nearly 200 meals out of vending machines. We spent nearly $900 on stamps. But all of those dollars and all of those hours were but a small portion of what Marty's sentence cost him and his family. He lost seven years of his life that he'll never get back. We lost seven years of having him with us.

Like the snowflakes that had pelted our windshield on our trip to Yankton, the years slowly melted. Marty had paid back society. We had also served our time.

Marty walked out of the prison camp carrying a couple of boxes. Seven years of his life were contained in those two cardboard boxes. But, there was more to him. He had earned two college degrees. He was committed to building a new, drug-free life. He now appreciated his family.

The depressing memories of Valentine's Day 2001 were all but erased. We could go on. We still don't know the reason for those past seven years, for everything. Our son is a man, a good man. He has a good job using his degree in horticulture. He has helped other ex-felons find employment. He attends a couple of Narcotics Anonymous meetings each week. Even though the Bureau of Prisons doesn't realize it, and I really hate to admit it, the bureau had helped our son grow. And us, we have also grown.

Ebonny Fowler

The Long Wait Home

I t's a cool October afternoon in New York City, three days before my fourteenth birthday. The year is 1989.

I'm looking up at my childhood hero—my big brother, Jamal. My face is lit up like a Christmas tree; I'm grinning ear to ear. Jamal has just told me he's going to get the latest Diadora sneakers for my birthday. Diadoras are some of the coolest kicks a girl can have on her feet in the Wagner projects of Harlem. I want my birthday to hurry up and come so I can show off my new sneakers and proudly tell all my friends, "My brother got these for me!"

It's not the thought of owning a new pair of sneakers that has me feeling exhilarated. It is the fact that my nineteen-year-old brother is once again filling the void left by my absent father.

Jamal is not only my big brother but also a father figure to me. I desperately need him.

As Jamal walks out the front door to meet up with his friends, I smile and tell him I can't wait until the big day. Three days seems like such a long time to wait.

～～

Jamal never made it home that night. He was wrongfully arrested for a crime he didn't commit and has spent the last twenty years in prison. I've been waiting for my brother to come back home for two decades—240 months; 7,306 days, and counting.

I'd give anything to have that day in 1989 back. I would've told Jamal that I didn't care about any material items, that all I really wanted—all I needed—was for him to always be there, showing me unconditional love.

Numerous events have passed while Jamal has been locked up. Our family has marked many birthdays, holidays, and family get-togethers without him. While my relatives and I wait for Jamal's return home, the telephone is the link that connects us. Those times when family members are gathered together, we anxiously await Jamal's phone call so we can take turns talking to him. Sometimes we hold the phone up in the air while we sing "Happy Birthday," so he can in some way join the celebration.

When my grandmother was diagnosed with pancreatic cancer, the family gathered at her apartment, held hands and prayed together. All of my immediate family members were joined in a circle, except my brother. Jamal had to listen through the phone. Granny was too ill to visit Jamal in prison, so his last conversations with the woman who was like a second mother to him were only through a wired connection.

The next time Jamal saw Granny was at her funeral. Jamal had to lean over her casket to say his final goodbyes while wearing shackles around his ankles. He had to wear shackles and handcuffs at our grandfather's funeral, too. He wasn't even allowed to attend our uncle's funeral service.

There have also been new additions to our family while Jamal has been in jail. My little cousins were born, and one of them is now a teenager preparing for college. I'm waiting for the day when my young cousins can see Jamal outside the confines of a prison visiting room.

For the last twenty years, I've been constantly waiting.

Waiting for the time of day Jamal is allowed to call home. Waiting for him to call back once we're disconnected because of the thirty-minute phone limit. Waiting for those days when Jamal is allowed to have visitors. Waiting for correctional officers to inspect the food, magazines, and clothes we bring for Jamal before they give them to him, and then waiting in lines to be processed for a visit.

Waiting every two years for Jamal's next parole board hearing.

Waiting for the parole board's decision.

Waiting for the board to grant parole to Jamal and not constantly deny him on the basis of "the nature of the crime."

Waiting for my brother to be exonerated.

I'm waiting for the day when I drive to a correctional facility for the last time, give my brother a long hug, and drive him home. I'm waiting for the huge family get-together celebrating Jamal's long-awaited return. I'm waiting to cry tears of joy and happiness to finally see my entire family together. I look forward to the day when Jamal can sing with us in person on every birthday, eat dinner with us on Thanksgiving, and open gifts with us on Christmas.

I'm waiting for Jamal to take the place of my absent father and walk me down the aisle on my wedding day. I'm waiting for the day when my future children and Jamal's future kids play together.

I'm still waiting for that new pair of shoes. But this time it will be a pair that I give my brother to proudly walk out of that correctional facility. I look forward to seeing the big smile on my mother's face as both her children walk into her house for the first time together in a long, long while.

I can't wait for my beloved brother to begin his new life as a free man.

Jason Dansby

Don't Go

I vividly remember that look my mother gave me when she told me that she had to leave our city of Asheville, North Carolina, and never return.

Accused of breaking into her parents' house and stealing checks from their checkbook, she disappeared from the neighborhood and from the minds of most people. But she never left the forefront of my mind. I would not let her.

At sixteen years old, I knew that the pain of losing her would reverberate the rest of my days.

The pain felt like a blade piercing my chest, even though I knew I should be used to her leaving by then.

The first time she went to prison, I was ten and did not know what was going on. All I knew was that my "mommy" was being stripped from me. Being a mama's boy, it hurt. This time I was well aware of what was going on, and why, but it still devastated me in a way that would immensely affect my life. I did not want to deal with the hurt any longer. I wanted to shake it, but I could not. The thought of her roaming the streets, using and abusing crack cocaine to escape her harsh reality, haunted me like a gruesome phantom.

One day, I heard a soft knock at the front door of my brother's apartment, where I had gone to live when my mother left. I paused the Nintendo 64 video game that I was playing and went to open the door. I thought that one of my hoodlum friends would be on the other side. To my amazement, it was my mother.

There she stood, dressed in the same rags that she was wearing the last time I'd seen her. She did not look healthy; her face was sunken from drug use. "Death warmed over" would be the term to describe her appearance. It was unbearable, but I had not seen her in months, and the son in me was thankful to see her, no matter her condition.

After the awkward silence, fueled by my amazement and disgust, I asked her to come into the apartment and have something to eat, even though the cupboards were nearly bare. She accepted my invitation.

Tears worked their way into the corners of my eyes. I was never the crying type, but there were tears that day. I stared at her. She looked so very bad, and I felt bad for her. This was the woman who gave me life. She named me, cared for me, sent me to day care, and loved me. Did she still love me? Did she want to get the help that she so truly needed so that we could be a family again? All these questions festered in my soul. I wanted to ask her, but I did not want to start chastising her for not being there for my siblings and me. All I wanted was my mother back healthy and safe.

"Give me a hug, baby," she demanded. I could not move. I did not know the person who was asking me for a hug, but I longed to hug the woman inside. I wanted to squeeze the woman who lay trapped in her addiction.

"It's me, Jason," she reassured. I came out of my trance and gave her a hug. As much as I wanted it to feel the same as it had in the past, it didn't. My embrace was weak. Hers felt strong, tight. I knew that she loved me, but I longed to ask: "Dammit, why did you choose that crap over your children? Over *me*, your baby!"

She released her hold on me. I could not look at this woman. She was not my mother, but she was. I hated the decisions that she had made, but I loved her to death. Every time she went to prison, I wished that I were being taken away, not she. I wanted to protect her from everything but, no matter how much I tried, I could not save her from the streets. I could not save her from herself. I felt powerless. I was unable to help my mother when she needed me the most. These were the thoughts that ignited my tears.

"It's okay, sweetie," she said, trying to console me. I knew that it was not going to be okay. When the police found her, she would be going to jail for a very long time. It was just a matter of time. It was bound to happen, and happen soon. The inevitability of it all was crippling.

She walked into the kitchen and looked into the refrigerator to find it almost empty. "You guys don't have any food?" she asked. I had been working at McDonald's full-time, but it was Thursday night. I wouldn't get paid until Friday afternoon. My brother and I would have to tough it out until then.

"Not until tomorrow," I said, still shocked at the fact that my mother was here.

She walked to the front door.

"I'll be back in a few minutes," she said. I did not believe her. I did not want her to go because I did not know when I would see her again. My entire life was nothing but memories of her leaving me, her coming up with excuses as to why she would not be home or why we did not have food for dinner. I was sick of the excuses. I was sick of her leaving me. I could not take it another time.

"Mama, please don't go!" I begged. The more I begged, the more the tears streamed down my face, into the corners of my mouth. Every word she used to assure me fell on deaf ears.

"I promise that I'll be back, Jay." She opened the door and quickly departed. I cried uncontrollably; my mom had gone and I thought she was never coming back. With her bouncing in and out of prison, I did not have a clue as to what my future would be without her. Despite all the times she'd left in the past, I still had dreams of her attending to my future children, her grandchildren, someday. I still had dreams of her making up for the time that she had lost because of the drugs, the stealing, and the manipulation. But when that door shut this time, all those dreams came to a crashing halt.

An hour and a half went by. I was alone in the apartment, still crying and worried. All I wanted was for my mother to come back. All I could think about was her being apprehended by the authorities and my never seeing her again. Then my worries turned to anger. Dammit, I thought, she lied to me, again. I was sick of being lied to by her. Maybe her being arrested would be the best thing for her; she'd be off the streets and in a place where she could get her priorities straight.

I felt like a bad son for thinking that. How could I wish prison on my own mother? How could I forsake her? How could I let her kill herself? I was torn between my thoughts and didn't know what to do. All I knew was that I loved my mother and that I would not call the police.

Then the door opened. It was my mother. I jumped up from the couch. I was so happy to see her, extremely happy to see that she had kept her promise. She'd returned, and hadn't come empty-handed. "Jay, I need your help," she said. She asked me to follow her.

I trailed her from our apartment to a vehicle with its trunk ajar. Inside the trunk were groceries—lots and lots of groceries. I took most of them in my arms while my mother retrieved the last bag. Maybe she is going to stay here, I thought.

That thought vanished when we got back to the apartment.

"Honey," she said.

"Yes, Mama."

"I have to go. The police are looking for me because I stole some checks. I don't want to go to jail, so I am going on the run."

"How long will you be gone, Mama?" I asked, my voice trembling with pain.

"I don't know, Jay. All I want you to know is that I will keep in contact with you and that I love you very much."

I looked down at the groceries that she had purchased.

"Why did you get these groceries?" I asked.

"I wanted to make sure that you and Rick had something to eat." She had used her last stolen check to buy us food. "Please don't tell your grandmother that I came by here."

"I don't want you to go," I told her. I started to cry again. I knew that her time was running short and that the police would capture her.

"I have to, baby," she said. "I want you to promise me that you will not tell Mom or Pop that you saw me, okay?"

I hesitated. My heart wanted to make that promise, but I did not want my mother to suffer the effects of drugs any longer. I did not want her to be a prisoner of her addiction. For so long, she had done everything that she could to support her habit, and it had imprisoned her. The proverbial chains were tight, shackling her to her dealer and his product.

"Promise me, Jay," she demanded.

"I … I promise," I said, lowering my head in shame. I was enabling her to kill herself. I should do exactly the opposite of what she is asking of me, I thought. I should call my grandmother and tell her that Mama is running.

She walked to the front door and opened it. "Don't ever forget that I love you, Jason. No matter what happens, always remember that."

The door slammed and she was gone.

～～

After that night, my life fell apart. My mother was eventually caught, charged with being a habitual offender for forgery, and sentenced to ten years. From the moment she said goodbye, I felt like I wanted to die. I felt as if a piece of me left with her that night. To this day, that piece of me has yet to fully return.

At the age of sixteen, I thought I'd lost what was the world to me, but I now realize I lost that when I was a child. I lost my mother, but I also lost my childhood.

I had recurring nightmares about her leaving me, nightmares that ended in devastating heartache. If it wasn't her being dragged away by the "pigs," it was her dying. I couldn't stand it. For months, it was hard for me to eat. For years, it was hard for me to sleep, and I was eventually diagnosed with sleep deprivation. Depression invaded my consciousness and took over my body. I would stay out as late as possible at night, not wanting to go home.

I quickly picked up the hobby of pushing drugs on the street corner. It started out as something that I really did not want to do, but I had a death wish. I did not want to be on this earth any longer, and suicide was not an option. I started out with fake crack—"dummies," as we called it in the ghetto—selling anything from candle wax to drywall. Customers bought it like hotcakes. By the time they realized that it was not the real thing, I had gone and was off counting my money. I sold the fake crack for enough money to get the real deal. I bought a quarter-pound of cocaine for cheap, and my cousin and I cooked it down into crack.

The money was great, and the life-threatening experience was a rush. Guns were a must at that point. My mother wasn't coming home anytime soon, and I just stopped caring. So I carried a gun with me at all times.

It was a guilty victory for me. Sitting in my room counting money that customers should have spent on their families, Christmas, birthdays, made the experience so appalling. I thought about the times when I looked into my mother's eyes, and I started to ponder the way I felt about the whole situation. I thought about the times when my mother was spellbound by the very filth that I was peddling on the street corner. I thought about those times when she pawned our belongings. We grew up with no phone, no cable, and sometimes no lights so Mama could get her fix. Our friends were afraid of spending the night with my brother and me. It made me so furious.

How could I be advertising the very same crap that put me in this predicament? How could I put some child through the situation that I had been through? I had to end this, but I was torn between the money and lifestyle, and the right thing to do. My heart was weighed down. Death seemed like the only way out.

I looked down at the gun I'd placed at my waist in case someone barged in to rob me. I picked it up and put it to my temple. I'd had enough of this life. I'd had enough of the pain. I'd had enough of the suffering. I'd had enough of people being taken away from me. If I were not alive, I wouldn't have to worry about all of this.

Just then, I started shaking like a leaf. For the first time since my mother was ripped from my life, I suddenly started to think rationally. *I can't do this! If I do this, then I will never see my mother again. These streets will have won the war that I have been waging all my life. I can't let that happen.*

From that moment forward, I put the crack away and stopped selling it.

I focused on music as my outlet. I wrote about the pain that I had suffered at the hands of the streets. My friends and I wrote music constantly; we were pretty talented, if I do say so myself. During this time, it really felt as if my life was getting back on track. But then yet another overwhelming blow happened.

~~

I was working at McDonald's with my two best friends on July 4, 1998. The sun shone bright as we looked forward to going downtown after work to enjoy the annual fireworks. Then the phone rang.

"McDonald's. How may I direct your call?" the manager asked. After a brief silence, she handed me the phone.

"Hello," I said. It was my grandmother. What was she doing calling me at work? She knew that my shift would end soon and that I would be stopping by her house to wish a happy Fourth of July to her, my oldest sister, Tia, and the family. She asked me to come home. I could hear the despair in her voice. Something was not right. I started to worry. "What's going on, Mama Ann?" I asked.

She simply kept repeating that I needed to come home. The son in me started to panic. Had something happened to my mother in jail? "Mama Ann, what's going on?" I asked again, this time with a stern voice that I hoped would prompt her to say whatever had her tongue-tied.

Abruptly, my sister Nikki took the phone from my grandmother. "You need to come home!" she said. "I am on my way to get you." With that, she hung up the phone.

What in the hell was going on? I waited five minutes, until I thought my sister had left, and called my grandmother back. When she picked up the phone, I heard my grandfather talking in the background, so I figured that whatever was going on didn't involve him. Since Nikki was on her way to pick me up, it had nothing to do with her. Mama was in jail, so that ruled her out. My brother's girlfriend, Stephanie, had not called, so it was not about my brother. The only one left was Tia.

"Mama Ann," I said softly, "what happened to Tia?"

My grandmother started to cry, and I knew that something had happened to my sister. Tia had told me two days earlier that she had to go to the hospital but didn't tell me why. I thought that it was for a routine check-up.

I glanced out the window to the McDonald's play area, where my best friend Josh was on his break. The sky looked sinister, with clouds rolling in.

"What happened, Mama Ann?" I asked again.

"Tia died today, Jason," she managed to say between sobs. At those words, the sky blackened. Thunder clapped ferociously. I began to cry hysterically. Another woman in my life had been taken away from me and there was nothing that I could do about it—again. I told my grandmother that I would be there as soon as Nikki came to get me.

Josh ran in from the play area and joined me behind the counter. My other friend, Kentell, finished with a customer then rushed to my side.

"What's going on, Jay?" Josh asked.

I looked at him and Kentell, but at first I couldn't get the words out of my mouth. I didn't want to believe that my sister was gone and was never coming back.

Finally, I muttered through my sobs, "Tia died!"

Josh and Kentell hugged me tightly. I needed them. I needed to be consoled. I needed to be told that it was going to be okay. I needed my mother.

~~~

After a year and a half of trials and tribulations, the millennium arrived. I made a resolution that 2000 was going to be a better year than years past. The Internet fame of my rap group, Prisoners of War, was rising, and I had met a girl named Tarah from Vermont. She was very interested in our music.

But I continued to live with guilt. My life was moving a mile a minute, and it was almost impossible to write my mother. I was seventeen years old. Women and sex consumed my lifestyle. I was too busy being a player to write my own mother. I only wrote her three times and never even attempted to visit her. I thought that I was a terrible son; I lived with that pain for a long time.

When Tarah's mother asked me to come and visit Vermont, I dropped everything and took the offer. I spent a week there. When I got back home to Asheville, I started talking to Tarah about moving up to Vermont. The thought of leaving Asheville and all the callous memories behind brought tranquility to my heart. And Tarah's mother thought it was a good idea. So, on June 28, 2000, I moved to Bennington, Vermont. My family asked, *"Why?"*

As it turned out, Bennington was a different type of drama. I did not have to deal with reminders of my mother or Tia anymore, but I was so homesick. I went through each day pretending that nothing was wrong, but everything was. The girl I'd moved over 800 miles for was cheating on me, repeatedly. *There's another female that I lost,* I thought to myself. I started to have a careless attitude.

In the summer of 2001, I was eighteen and getting back my lost teen years. At the time, I was moving from pillar to post, not knowing where I would eat my next meal. I started running with a girl and some friends who were cashing the girl's checks and buying anything we wanted, smoking weed, and partying all the time. The only thing was that her bank account had been empty for months. One of these friends got arrested, and then the girl got arrested, and then me and a few others. We were charged with "false token/false pretenses (bad checks)." With additional charges of obstruction of justice and perjury, I served two years before getting out on probation.

I had met someone and gotten married, and we were expecting a baby, when I lost yet another important individual in my life. My grandfather Ernest died. He'd really been the father in my life. It hurt me deeply; I wanted him to be there to see my children. I wanted my children to know him and to love him the way that I did, and still do.

Then I violated probation and was sent back to jail for another twenty-four months. During this time in jail, I had an enormous weight on my shoulders. I had a pregnant wife and stepchildren waiting for me to get out of prison. That made the jail time worse. When you have people like that to worry about, you can kiss your sanity goodbye.

For the first year of my incarceration, my wife was faithful; she visited regularly and often sent letters and pictures. When our first son, Dejaun, was born, she brought him to visit me. I still remember seeing him for the first time. I walked into the visiting room and saw my wife holding our son in her arms with a blanket over his face. When she uncovered his face, his big eyes batted at me. I cried, instantly. I cried at the thought that I could be responsible for helping to make something so pure and innocent. I cried because I was not there to cut his umbilical cord.

After I was sentenced and sent out of state, my wife became unfaithful. That pain cut like an axe, burying its sharp head in my chest, stopping my heart from loving. I'd lost another woman in my life.

I was let out again. My wife became pregnant with our second child, but our relationship was breaking apart. I started seeing another woman, who became pregnant. After a few months, I was sent back to jail and told I had to finish thirty-six months because the Vermont Department of Corrections had made a mistake in my sentence.

This time in prison, however, a pattern has been broken. I have been in a committed relationship with a woman whom I love very much—and she has not left.

I continued to have contact with my mother by sending letters to my grandmother, who would send them to her. Mama was very supportive of me, even when I became depressed about my situation. I told her how I was the "chip off the old block." I felt as though I had let her down. My whole life, my mother has been my world. Whenever anyone said that she was doing wrong, I challenged every word. I remember my grandmother saying, "You must really love your mama because you take up for her through anything." My mother had been the woman I always wanted to turn to for advice or suggestions on anything, but I was never given the opportunity until now. After serving ten years, she is in the community—and doing well.

Sometimes I lie in my bunk and think of the possibility of her turning back to the old lifestyle that she knew for years. I wonder if her ten-year confinement was the thing that she needed to put her life in perspective. My grandmother always brings up the fact that she's old. Death is inevitable; one day Mama Ann will be called back to the Lord. I wonder if my mother is ready to take over the role Mama Ann has played—of hosting the Christmas and Easter get-togethers, the cookouts.

Are you ready for that, Mama? Being a mama's boy, I have all the faith in the world in you. I have all the love in the world for you. Thank you for giving me life. Thank you for giving me love. I know that I was not the best son to you, and that I should have written more and done more. For years I have waited for you to get out of prison. Now that you are out, the roles have reversed and you are waiting for me. Thank you for waiting. Thank you for giving me hope. Thank you for giving me you. With all my heart, I love you, Mama!

Ninowtzka Mier

A Change of Plans

*B*oom. *Boom. Boom.* Thunderous pounding echoed over and over at the door of my family's hotel room at Disney World. Before my father could open the door, an FBI agent wearing a light blue Mickey Mouse jacket swung it open. Another agent was close behind. They threw my father to his knees. Towering over him, they pointed a gun to his head and handcuffed him. Life, as my family knew it, was over.

I was eighteen, had just graduated from high school and was about to begin classes at Florida International University. I was excited about the future and looked forward to studying journalism, theater, and English literature. I had a talent for writing and college would be my chance to study my first love. I worked at Chess King, a men's clothing store, but the job was temporary; I wanted to embark on a writing career.

But my lovely ideas about my future vanished the day the FBI agents stormed into our lives and I saw my father with a gun to his head. I screamed for my dad while two other agents, a tall man and a blonde woman, grabbed my two younger sisters and me. These agents wore black clothing with the letters FBI in white. The woman had wavy, shoulder-length hair. Though when I think back, their faces are always a blur. But I'll always remember what my father was wearing as he knelt with a gun to his head: light yellow pants and a worn white polo shirt with light blue stripes running across it. It was what he typically wore when relaxing at home or on vacation. It was the fastest thing he could throw on when he heard the pounding at the door.

The agents forced us into the bathroom. I held my sisters, rocking them both as I cried. They were ten and seven. I was grateful they had not witnessed our father's arrest as I had. I peeked out of the bathroom and watched the agents question my stepmother. They looked down at her and chuckled at every answer she gave to their questions. It seemed like a game where the intention was to ridicule and humiliate the family after their protector was snatched away. The agents reminded me of the way hyenas cackle while they feast on the remains of their kill.

The agents confiscated our SUV, so we had to rent a car to get home, almost four hours away. I stared out the passenger window and cried most of the drive home.

I could not see my father for three months, not until Christmas 1994. He was in a prison an hour from our home. As I approached the prison, a little girl with brown curly hair ran past me to reach the entrance; the ruffles on her yellow dress bounced with each stride. Her mother followed her at a slower pace. A prison guard, a lean woman wearing a starched white short-sleeved shirt and grey pants, adorned with a holster and, on each shoulder, prison guard badges, yelled at the little girl, "Turn back around and walk back!"

Stunned, I watched the child's smile fade. She turned somber and stopped in her tracks, as if she'd struck an invisible wall. She obeyed the orders. She walked back the same way she had come, only to make the same trip back in a slow march. When she walked past me, I noticed a small sign stabbed into the grass: "Walk. Do Not Run."

As if I were not nervous enough already, I worried whether there were other signs I may have missed on the way from the parking lot, like, "Smiling is Frowned Upon," "Breathe at Your Own Risk," or "Avoid Facial Expressions." I hoped I had not disobeyed anything because I would have crumbled if I had received the harsh treatment the little girl endured. I probably would have appreciated signs like "Prepare to Be Questioned, Scrutinized and Mocked," "Your Wait Time Will Always Be Longer Than Expected," or "Question Nothing."

During the fifteen-minute call to the house he was permitted the night before, my father prepared me for my visit. He educated me about the dress code: long pants, sleeved top, nothing revealing or suggestive, sneakers or tennis shoes but no black boots or khakis, or anything resembling the inmates' uniforms. Any cash was to be carried in a zip-lock bag, no bills larger than twenties. No cell phones.

I walked through the visitors' doors and entered a room filled with families waiting to see their loved ones. I filled out the paperwork required for entry, and I waited. Looking back on it all now, it seems that all I did then was wait. I waited at the prison, waited by the phone for the brief phone calls, waited for an answer from the court, waited to hear from the lawyer, and just waited for my dad to come home—nearly thirteen years of agonizing waiting.

My father's absence took its toll on family life. We struggled financially. I was grateful I still had my job at Chess King. Eventually, I was promoted to assistant manager and the money I earned went toward household bills and college, whatever my loans could not cover. I tried to manage my father's business affairs, but once his business partners learned he was away, the money my father earned stopped coming in. My stepmother worked multiple jobs.

My sisters were growing up without their father. We missed him; we needed him home. It was clear that he was the glue that kept us together. Without him, family life became more and more volatile. I argued with my stepmother more frequently. My middle sister, who'd just turned fourteen, was growing up without any guidance. I thought I could offer some, but she and my stepmother resisted that idea. My wondering where my fourteen-year-old sister was at 3:00 a.m. would immediately spark an argument between my stepmother and me. She did not instill discipline or boundaries the way my father did, and my father asked me to intercede whenever I could. That, of course, caused problems; my stepmother accused me of spying for my father. I was alone and powerless.

My younger sister, Helen, suffered in silence. She really needed him most of all. She had a disability that prevented her from learning as quickly as other children. She was much like a child, even as a teenager. My father was the family's stabilizer and Helen's beacon, infinitely patient and giving her the extra attention she needed. Even after an exhausting day on the job, he worked with Helen on her letters, word pronunciations, and math equations.

My father just kept getting farther away from us. He was transferred from facility to facility, sometimes as far as four states away from Florida. Visiting him was hard on the family.

The wait time was so long in one particular prison that families waited in line as early as the night before. My sisters and I would arrive at the facility at 2:00 a.m. carrying our blankets and pillows. We'd take our place in line among the other bundled families, and sleep on the sidewalk until doors opened at 7:00 a.m. Then, the real wait would begin. We would fill out visitation papers, ready photo identifications, and prepare for transfer to another waiting room where, again, we waited. When we were finally in the visiting room, we waited for my dad to arrive.

I came to expect to be treated like a criminal in most of these facilities. The few places where the guards treated my family with respect were the exceptions and not the rule. Even when I thought I was being treated with respect and dignity, something would instantly bring me back to the reality that I was in a prison.

I recall one of our visits that was interrupted because it was time for "the count," when every inmate is counted. Each guard had his or her own way of conducting the count. Sometimes it lasted no more than a few minutes, other times it was a drawn-out process. This time, my father walked out of the line where the guards were counting. He had been counted and thought it was permissible to rejoin me at our table. He was wrong. A guard who had always shown my father and me respect and consideration scolded him as if he were a child. This young man shouted at my father—an educated and accomplished man, whom I admired and adored—for daring to disobey his command. The happiness I'd felt during the visit was over, as I found myself witnessing a public admonishment of a disobedient prisoner by the ever-powerful prison guard. I know it crushed and humiliated my father, but he never showed it. He apologized to the guard, smiled, and returned to our table when he was told to do so. I was never pleasant to that guard again.

Over the years I learned how to be independent and rely on myself. My relationship with my stepmother remained strained, and she divorced my father ten years after he was arrested. Though I wanted to become a writer, I decided to pursue a law degree. Part of me wanted to crack the "lawyer code" that was always thrown at us when discussing my father's case and what we should expect. I was tired of relying on attorneys to tell me what was happening. I wanted answers, and law school helped me realize how convoluted the legal system can be. I was sad to let go of my dream of becoming a writer. I consoled myself by believing that I could always be a writer after law school. I promised I would not allow law school to "kill my soul," as one poetry professor thoughtfully put it when he warned me against law school.

My father served twelve years, eight months for money laundering. This was a short reduction of his initial fourteen-year sentence under the existing Federal Sentencing Guidelines. The guidelines gave no consideration to mitigating factors, like the fact that he was a first-time offender, or that his was a nonviolent crime, or that his family needed him home.

My younger sister, Helen, did not live to see the day when our father returned home. She died one month after being diagnosed with leukemia, a few years before his release. His warden showed compassion and allowed him to attend her funeral. I will never know how it felt for my father when he could not be by her side in her last days. I know that he never imagined burying any of his children.

By the time my father returned home, everything was different. He had no wife, had lost his youngest daughter, and had to start his life over at the age of fifty-eight. Before he went away, he had an air of confidence that made him larger than life. He was charismatic, compassionate, and witty. After he served his time, he was thinner, older, and tired. And, I imagine, heartbroken.

He brought back some interesting skills he learned in prison; for example, he showed me his new method to recharge batteries: take two batteries—AA or AAA work the best—and microwave them on high for two minutes. Good as new. He chuckled as he showed me. Moments like that reassured me that prison did not completely rob him of his spirit and humor.

My family and I endured unimaginable challenges when my dad's deeds, the laws, the agents, the judicial system, and the guidelines took him away from us. Today, he struggles each day to get back on his feet. He works for minimum wage, parking cars at an airport. As his daughter, a lawyer, and a citizen of this world, I recognize that he made a mistake. He was judged and served an inordinate amount of time for a nonviolent crime.

I wonder what good it served to have my father imprisoned. I am unable to come up with one positive aspect of having him locked up, except that his presence kept prison guards employed and aided arguments for the need for more prisons.

When I think about how it failed to serve society, I am overwhelmed. My father became a burden on taxpayers. His marriage failed. His daughters grew up without their father. He can no longer vote. He has no voice in shaping the nation's future, including sharing his invaluable insight on the effects of mandatory minimum prison sentences. He will forever be judged for any future employment or opportunities as simply a convicted felon.

Ashley White

A Typical Saturday

Saturday morning, almost 3:00 a.m.

I didn't forget to bring my pillows and blankets this time. It's dark and creepy in this parking lot. The high wall is enough to scare you. There's one bright light shining from the tower at me—right in my eyes through my windshield.

I'm trying to get some sleep before they come around with the numbers at 7:15 a.m. I'm here to see my husband, the man who truly changed my life, and the man I truly adore.

The visits don't start until 9:00 a.m. But if you want to get in then, you have to be here before 7:15 a.m. to get a number before all the free buses bring friends and loved ones in from New York City. Otherwise, you'll be waiting a very long time to get in. I try to get comfortable in my car, but it's just not working, and the sounds of all the cars that pull up next to mine awaken me. Eventually, we all line up next to each other to get a number. I pray that no fights start and that people don't try to cut in line. We see the official van drive up, and we know that we're about to get our numbers.

Numbers in hand, we leave and get some breakfast, coming back around 8:30 a.m. to hop on the van and sign in at the visiting center. We either wait in the visiting center until our numbers are called, or we go wait in our cars. It's loud in the center, and all the different smells in the air—breakfast food, lotions, hairsprays, perfumes—make my stomach turn, so usually I wait in my car. They call the numbers in blocks of five—one to five, six to ten, etc. They take forever. As the minutes pass, I get so antsy about seeing my husband.

They cram us in the van to go from the visiting center to the main entrance of the facility. The heat is usually cranked up; with everyone crowded on top of each other, it's even more uncomfortable.

Ah, relief! I get off the van, and I go and wait in yet another room. The guard at the front desk is so rude. I show my ID and hand in my visitor's slip. I then sit and wait for them to call my name. As others are called before me, I pray that they don't set off the metal detector—beep, beep, beep. I hear that noise in my dreams. The guards bark, "Take your bra off! Do you have an underwire on? Go in the bathroom and take it off." I come prepared and make sure I have no metal on; it just holds up the line. I'm familiar with the drill because, unfortunately, this isn't my first prison experience. But I never saw myself in this scenario again.

They call me. I go right through. After they look through my stuff, they stamp my right hand, and I go through another gate. I get to the next door, where they check my slip again. Another gate takes me to the visiting room to the left. As I walk toward it, I see a few guards staring me down; I stare right back. When I enter the visiting room, five guards are standing there, and two are sitting at the desk. It's very intimidating.

"Hello," I say. Sometimes I get no response. They're not very friendly individuals.

"You're sitting in five-two," the guard says.

"Okay, thank you," I say.

As I wait for my husband, I go to the vending machines. Great, this machine isn't taking $1s or quarters. Now what? The food is horrible. I get what I can, then sit down to wait for him.

At this point, I'm beat. I got up at 1:00 a.m. I left my house at 2:00 a.m. I'm just about to shut my eyes when I see his face coming through the heavy metal door that slams behind him.

He looks at me and smiles. I don't know how to feel at this point. I'm happy to see him, but sick of all this crap I have to go through to get in here to see him for six hours a week. We sit next to each other, hold hands, and briefly kiss. All we can do is talk and fantasize about when he comes home. The room gets really hot and stuffy, and the air fills with smells of a mixture of different foods being heated in the microwaves.

It's so loud; I unintentionally get pulled into other people's conversations. I can't concentrate. I start fights with my husband because I just can't act "normal" in here. I laugh, and then I cry.

The guards constantly stare at us visitors; they snicker and even make rude comments just to keep us from visiting. We can't let them intimidate us and beat us. That is what they want.

When it's time to go, we say goodbye. We visitors gather in the front of the visiting room while the inmates remain seated at the tables until we leave the room. That is the hardest part for me. I hate coming in, and I hate leaving him there.

I married my husband three days before he got locked up, innocent of the crime he was convicted of. I had a choice; I could stay with him and ride this out, or I could leave and forget about him. I stayed. He got nine years.

With God's help, I'll make it through this rough time. I love him! With the support of friends and family, I know we can make it through this. No steel bars can break our love. I'll endure as many typical Saturdays as I have to until he comes home.

Jennifer Collins

The Long Road Home

The umbilical cord between us,
Invisible to the naked eye,
Has a life of its own.
No matter how hard I try
To pull away, even at my age,
It has an elastic snap
And cuts me short, then bounces
Me back to you.

I wonder how long it spans,
Even as you get carted away,
Across highways,
Somewhere upstate,
I know I will feel the internal tug,

Pull and tug and pull,
Till the pain brings tears to my eyes,
And I run to the kitchen to grab hold
Of the scissors to cut and cut and cut
Me away from you.

But no matter how hard I try,
The damn thing finds its ways back
And re-attaches itself to my heart,
To my gut—to your beating belly center
From which it was born.

It has been four years since the incident involving my mother and her partner. I say incident because I still find it difficult, even after all this time, to say that my mother is incarcerated for attempted murder.

April 13, 2005, was the day our lives changed. I was on my way to work when I received a frantic phone call from my grandmother urging me to come home—something terrible had happened and the police were at the house. I had no idea what to expect. How could I have known that when I turned the corner, headed toward home, the streets would be lined with police cars and yellow tape would be encircling my house?

I remember my feelings. Nothing looked real. It was as if I were looking at a scene in a movie and, suddenly, I was the guest star walking onto the set. All eyes were on me as I hesitantly walked toward the driveway to speak to a police officer. The officer was reluctant to let me into the house because it was a crime scene, but my grandparents were inside. They were confused, crying, and unable to make heads or tails of what my mother had done or what would happen next. I remember hearing, "She stabbed her. She stabbed her."

So that's how it was. My mother stabbed her—four or five times, maybe more. No one knew if her partner was going to make it. The ambulances came and took them away, separately, to the same hospital.

That's how my nightmare began. I was thirty-five years old, married, a recent social work graduate, with two bewildered grandparents in their eighties, no siblings to whom I could turn for help or advice on what to do, where to turn, or how to proceed. I called relatives and friends, and I turned to my husband, who was just as confused and stunned as me.

I sobbed; I screamed and slammed my fists on the table. Then I got dizzy and felt nauseated. The air felt thin and my breath was uneven. I wanted to die; I wanted to crawl under a rock and never come out.

The house was in disarray, but it had been that way before this happened, right? So I tried to remember what the day before had been like, and the day before that, and the day before that one, too. But I couldn't. All I knew was that I was upstairs standing in the hallway near my mother's bedroom, staring at the pool of blood, still wet on the white carpet.

⌒〜⌒

I remember standing in line outside Nassau County Jail, waiting to see my mother for the first time since the incident. I noticed the faces of people next to me, who were also waiting to see their loved ones. They were doing time just like me. I stood in line with them outside the jail, feeling tired and anxious. My heart, as if it weighed 100 pounds, dropped to the floor so many times I could feel a hollow empty space where it belonged.

I never thought I'd find myself here, counting the minutes outside a jail. Each and every moment was a struggle to stay afloat. I felt alone in a sea of foreign objects without a lifesaver. I didn't know if I would sink or have the strength to swim to shore. I remember feeling so out of place. Nothing was familiar. It was as if I had landed in a new country unable to speak the language.

All things dangerous are creeping in,
the light under the door casts shadows
that linger in the dark,
like never before,
places in my soul that should never
be touched by this
cold steel blade—
voices crying out
for healing the dark places,
the broken spaces
in our souls.

I know in my heart that my mother is not a criminal or a violent person, even though she committed a horrendous act. My mother had a psychotic break with reality and lost all judgment. At least that's the way I saw it. She was absolutely not herself.

When I think about the charitable and honorable life my mother and her partner built for themselves, I feel crushed to think how one moment of instability and pure insanity shook and broke our family tree. What are we now? A bunch of fallen branches? It was not supposed to be this way.

Where will we go from here? I am so afraid. I am afraid of losing my mother and my family. The little girl in me wants her mother to come home; the adult in me just wants to save her.

I think of my mother's partner and my heart aches. I feel so much pain. She was in my life since I was nine years old, and now she feels so far away. How will she heal from this? How will her life be? What will become of all of us?

Some people believe that things happen for a reason, and that the Universe or God knows best. But what could be the reason for this, and where is God now?

~

Today, I think about all that has changed and how life has evolved while we've all been waiting anxiously for my mother's return, waiting for the dark clouds to lift, and to feel the sun's warmth on our cold, tired bodies. While we've waited, there have been breaks in the clouds and the sun has shone through. My husband and I welcomed our first child into our lives, filling my grandparents with new hope and joy. But then last year, there was the passing of my grandfather. My family and I had feared that he would not be here when my mother returned from prison. She was granted a bedside visit, and she was able to spend time with him. I think they got the closure they needed. But I also know that saying goodbye that way was excruciating for my mother. She was, however, grateful to have been able to see him alive one last time, rather than in a box.

That April day in 2005 seems like a lifetime ago. It feels as if I've served two or more life sentences. In the beginning, it was torture. I didn't know how I was going to make it through the next day, the next hour, or even the next breath. But it was breaths—through my yoga practice—that helped me cope and helped me get through each moment, each hour, each day. I allowed the inhalations and exhalations to come and go, and I was able to be present to all that was happening. I let myself scream and cry and break things. I allowed myself to feel the pain, the anger, the sadness, the loss and, mostly, the uncertainty. Yoga has helped me to breathe through the difficult and challenging moments of my life.

My mother is scheduled to come home later this year. I started out waiting for her like a bird on a perch—still, watchful, uneasy. I was afraid to use my voice to sing. I was afraid to fly, as if I had committed the crime myself, as if my own wings were clipped, as if I were chained and bound by her actions.

Having to shoulder the responsibility for someone else's mistakes is not an easy thing to do. You get mixed up in the pain and the love, and they often blur together, leaving you questioning and confused. Now, after four years of waiting, of mulling over, of taking care of her things—her parents, her home, her bills, her everything—I can finally say, "Enough!"

I have to get on with my life and believe that there is a light at the end of the tunnel, even though the road feels long and uncertain.

I love my mother and I look forward to having her back home, back in society. I've tried to picture her getting her life back together, feeling strong again, and being better than before. But I don't know if that will happen. I don't know what it will be like the day I pick her up and take her back home. I know that it will be a very emotional day for both of us. It will be the first time in five years that I will hug her outside of prison. Life will never be as it was before she went away. It can't possibly be; but with love and hope in our hearts, the future can look promising again.

Delores Mariano

Fear at the Gate of Release

As I sit and look out at the fences that once held me, I remember the waiting, the calling of my name and prison number for release. I had paid my dues, done my time, and then the day had come for me to walk—or wheel, should I say—through the gate in those fences.

My heart pounded that day, and my heart is pounding this day, for I am on the freedom side of the fences waiting for my daughter to walk out through that same gate. Those fences hold more than the body. They hold the soul of a person—the mind and every thought and hope of real freedom.

My daughter has had a drug addiction since she was fifteen years old—that was fifteen years ago. She informed me of this long addiction in a letter. How do I deal with her and her addiction? I learned how to separate myself from my addiction and leave it behind in the gutter, but has she been able to do the same for her life? I don't know. I have a fear of seeing her, of expecting change and getting nothing but the same old behavior, the same old garbage pouring out of her mouth, out of her very soul.

I had to take custody of her baby daughter, only a few months old. First, the baby's father went to prison for not completing a drug program. Then, my daughter went back because of a violation that she could have avoided.

"Let go of the street life and its ways," I cried to her. "You don't have to protect anyone but yourself."

As usual, she would not listen. A toy gun and a knife in the car, both belonging to her homeboy, got charged to her. So she was sent away for a longer time than necessary.

I sit and stare at that gate and those fences that have held her all these months. I wonder how she will be when she walks through the gate. Will there be the hateful yelling, and the pushing away of the baby she can't deal with? Or will she have truly changed? Will she be able to demonstrate heartfelt love and acceptance of her child? Will she learn to care for and love the child who looks at her pictures and calls out "Mama?" I wonder.

⁂

Here she comes. My heart races; I am actually scared to death. I don't want her to come through that gate. Hey, someone stop her; drag her back in, my mind screams.

But she's through the gate and almost at the car. My other daughter takes the baby to meet her. My newly released daughter hugs her sister and picks up her baby, who cries out "Mama."

My face smiles that expected smile of "Welcome home." But we both know this is not even close to a welcome home—it is more "Please stay here and away from me." I force the fear down.

I watch her approach the car. Her face reveals no real emotion—no tears, just that empty stare. She looks as though she knows she is somewhere else but does not know what to do with her new surroundings. Her look telegraphs that she is the same as before—bipolar. I remember the arguments and disagreements we had about her medications. Her illness could be controlled by taking two lousy pills a day. She refuses to take them; she denies she has a problem.

My heart is pounding with each step she takes.

She climbs into the car and starts yelling in my ear: She "hates" me; I am "rotten;" she "can't wait to get home" and "get away" from me. She says she is going to her friends, where she knows she is wanted.

All the money we sent to her, the letters she wrote saying she's sorry, the visit I fought to get to see her, even though my record would have normally prohibited it—all forgotten.

Nothing matters to her except the fact that I was a lousy mother and her addiction and incarceration are both my fault. It is the same thing all over again.

Being bipolar can keep people in addiction, in a private prison of mental torture. And women in prison are often not given the right medication for their illness; some with mental disorders have been given a drug that causes spontaneous abortion. My daughter was one of these women, not knowing she was pregnant until she aborted.

Yes, my daughter has been through a lot, but I can't feel for her. All I hear and see is someone who needs help and can't get it; someone who needs help and won't reach out and take it; someone who will blame someone else for the rest of her life and not take responsibility for her own actions.

Our family will suffer along with her, unless I separate us from her and let her go her own way. I live in fear that, once again, she comes through that gate maybe worse for the treatment she received and did not receive.

I will give her this last ride home. Then it is up to her to not get behind those fences and that gate again. I will not be here waiting on the outside, tearing my heart out in love and getting hatred in return.

Her madness and my fear accompany my beloved daughter whom I love with all my heart and wish she could love me back—or at least love her daughter, whom she pushes aside as she goes out the door to the gangsters in the streets who, she says, "love me so much."

~

She was on the way to her homeboy's house the other night when someone came up to him in the driveway and emptied the clip of a gun into him. Payback for deeds done in the past caught up with him, and almost with my daughter, who had done nothing to deserve payback for those deeds.

May he rest in peace and may she learn to change her ways before death catches up with her. My fear of my daughter's release from that prison gate is now fear of the unknown on the streets.

I hate this lifestyle she has chosen. She cannot even see what it holds for her.

Randy Peters

The Call

Donna sits in her simple farmhouse kitchen staring at the phone, willing it to ring. The green plastic on her metal dining room chair creaks as she shifts her weight from side to side. She wrings her hands, gets up, paces to the white refrigerator then back, sits down, and becomes mesmerized by her red cell phone lying on the old hardwood table. She twirls a finger in her thick auburn hair. It's a nervous childhood habit she's recently picked up again. Behind her, an antique faucet drips into its white basin, set in the center of a plain wooden counter. Dirty dishes line the black and green Formica top like forgotten soldiers. Donna's been waiting five years for this call, but the last three hours seem to take even longer. Her bright blue eyes are dulled with worry. She longs to hear her husband's voice telling her to come get him. Telling her the state is finally letting him come home.

Randy's sex crime conviction carried a rather complicated sentence of seven to forty years, all suspended, but with five years to serve. During incarceration, he has volunteered for and completed sex-offender therapy with the devotion of a Buddhist monk. Knowing he has serious problems, Randy has done his best to correct them. When the Department of Corrections releases him, he'll begin outpatient therapy once a week, see a probation officer once a week, keep a job, pay for therapy, pay for supervision, and cover his bills. The state adds to the pressure by not allowing him to drive for the first thirty days. It's going to be hard, but he and Donna have conquered tough times before. All they need to do is stick together.

Donna jumps when her "Smoke on the Water" ringtone vibrates the phone across the table. She scrambles to catch it before it crashes to the hardwood floor. Her heart skips a beat as she snaps open the phone.

"Hello?"

"Hi, Donna, whatcha doin'?"

"Hi, Mom. I'm waiting for Randy to call."

"Is today the day?"

"It sure is. Five years of hell almost over. There were times when I thought I'd die of a broken heart."

"You two have been through a lot. I remember how upset you were when they shipped him off to Oklahoma without telling anybody."

"I almost flipped. I drove for two hours to visit him, only to find out he wasn't in St. Albans and no one knew where he was."

"How long did you have to wait before he contacted you?"

"A week. I made dozens of calls to different jails and nobody would tell me anything. I wound up drinkin' again, 'cause I just couldn't handle the worry."

"You're a better woman than I am. I don't think I could've stuck it out if I was in your shoes."

"He's a good man, Mom. He treats me better than anyone ever has. He struggles with his demons, just like everybody else. His are more powerful and hurtful than most is all."

"I noticed a change in you from the first day you met him. Your whole outlook on life seemed to brighten."

"He sure has been good for me. I can't wait to have him home. Mom, I don't mean to be rude, but I don't wanna tie up the line. It's hard for Randy to get to a phone and I don't wanna miss his call."

"Okay, let me know if you need a ride to go get him."

"I will. Thanks. Bye, Mom; love you."

"I love you, too. Bye."

Donna sets her phone on the table and drifts to the sink. She plucks a large drinking glass from the cupboard overhead. Her hands shake as she reaches to fill it. Her glass clatters against the faucet then falls, shattering with a low pop.

"Damn it, damn it, damn it. I can't believe I just did that."

She grabs a square brown garbage pail from beside the stove on her left then pins it between her belly and the sink. One by one, Donna picks razor-sharp glass spears out of the basin and drops them in the bucket. After putting the trash can back, she collapses into her chair and runs a hand through her hair.

"I'm gonna be so glad when this is over. C'mon, Bear, call me."

Donna gets up and paces some more. Loose floorboards creak in tune with her tread. She shakes her hands and bounces on her toes. Three long, slow breaths calm her heartbeat. Wandering into the living room, she settles onto the blue cloth couch, picks up the remote, and turns on the TV. While a commercial for headache medicine squawks away, her mind floats back to when she first met Randy.

<center>~~~</center>

One warm summer morning, Donna had been riding to work with her husband at the time, and older sister. She sat in the passenger seat, arguing with him and yelling and waving her hands in frustration—he wanted to drop her off and take her black Chevy van touring for the day. Sporting greasy black hair, Greg was fat and lazy. He wouldn't find a job but had no problem spending her money. Donna was tired of his spending everything she earned.

She looked up ahead and saw a reddish orange Toyota pickup on the side of the road.

"Hey, isn't that the guy who hangs out with Eddie?" she said.

Greg grumbled, "Looks like 'im, so what?"

"Well, stop and see if he needs a ride, dummy."

"No."

"Whaddya mean, no? It's my van, and I say stop."

"Fine, whatever, as long as it shuts ya up."

Greg pulled over behind the truck and leaned out his window. "Hey, ya need a ride?"

A short, stocky man in a sleeveless t-shirt and old jeans peered out from under the hood. "Yeah, I do. I think my fuel pump's shot and I'm gonna be late for work."

"Where ya work?"

"Morrisville."

"Hop in; we're goin' right through there."

"Hey, thanks."

Donna climbed out of the passenger seat to get into the back beside her sister. Randy closed his hood, reached into the truck, and pulled out a red and white Igloo cooler. He jumped in the van, pushed up the brim of his ball cap, and scanned the rear seat. His eyes locked Donna's; her heart stopped. He had the most amazing hazel eyes she had ever seen.

~~~

The ringtone snaps her back to reality. Donna springs off the couch and trots to the kitchen. She can't get there fast enough; it's as if she's running in molasses. She snags the phone off the table on its third ring. "I hope this is Randy." She pops it open. "Hello?"

"Hi; is Jeremy there?"

Donna's hope collapses. She grits her teeth, shaking in frustration. "You have the wrong number; there's no Jeremy here."

"Oh, sorry."

Donna slams the phone shut, fighting an urge to heave it across the room. "Damn idiots. Can't even dial a friggin' phone right."

She squeezes it until her knuckles turn white. After another set of calming breaths, she forces herself to gently place the phone back on the table, marches to the window, and stares out into the distance. Across the blacktop road is a huge hayfield that borders a swale next to a fallen down barn, its flaking, red paint a memorial to days gone by. Anxiety gnaws at her gut as she chews her bottom lip and closes her gritty eyes. She breaks into a cold sweat when the phone breaks the silence. Two short steps bring her to the table. She lifts the phone and takes a deep breath. "Hello?"

"Hey, babydoll."

She flops into a chair; it slides backward a foot. Her held breath puffs out like a hurricane. "Oh-h-h, honey, I am so glad to hear from you. What the hell took so long? When can I come get you?"

"Well—um—they wouldn't let me call until they got done diddlin' with some paperwork."

"Does that mean you're set to come home?"

"No, uh—there's a problem."

Her heart stops and she can't breathe. "What kind of problem?"

"Aw-w-w, baby, this really sucks; I'm sorry."

"What's going on?"

"Probation decided not to let me go home. I gotta find another place to live."

"Why? What happened?"

"They decided eight-tenths of a mile isn't far enough from the school."

"But you finished the program. You didn't get in any trouble."

"I know, but evidently it don't mean shit. Nothin' I did is worth a damn."

"Your public defender said you could come home after five years."

"They changed the rules since then."

"They can't do that."

"They're not supposed to, but they did."

"What about the eighteen months you spent here during your trial? Not a single complaint from anybody. You didn't cause any trouble."

"It doesn't matter. Ever since what's-his-name killed that little girl, they're not letting any of us out."

"But that's not fair. You worked so hard. Damn it, I want you home. I'm sick of bein' lonely."

"Me, too, babe."

Hot tears run down Donna's face. Her hand shakes and her voice trembles as she asks, "What do we do now?"

"I gotta find some place else to go."

"Where?"

"Somewhere away from people."

"Well, what exactly are we supposed to look for?"

"I don't know. My P.O. says she don't have no set guidelines, just that I gotta live where she says."

"Then they should help us find a place."

"They ain't gonna. We gotta do it ourselves."

"Damn it, how much more of this shit have we gotta put up with?"

"I dunno. I got a feelin' they're gonna keep me in as long as they can."

A static-filled, electronic voice breaks in. "You—have —one—minute—remaining."

Fiery anger builds inside Donna's chest. "I hate these friggin' phones," she cries. "Do you have any more debit money so you can call me back?"

"No. I was expectin' to be right off, so I didn't buy any."

"That's just friggin' great."

"I'm sorry, baby."

"It's not your fault, Bear. I'm just really hurt and let down by all this shit."

"Me, too. I wanna say love you 'fore they shut us off, and I'll call as soon as I can."

Donna's gut-wrenching sobs steal her voice. Panic builds in Randy's mind. He remembers an earlier bout of depression that drove her to a suicide attempt.

"Baby? Baby, are you okay?"

Heartless, robotic words cut into his frantic scramble for reassurance. "Thank you for using—P.C.S.—please try again later."

Unable to contain her painful anger any longer, Donna heaves her phone against the wall; it shatters into pieces. She jumps up, toppling her chair, grabs the table, and upends it. She grabs her fallen seat and pounds it into the cupboard. Wood splinters and a hinge breaks free, leaving its door hanging askew. Donna swipes the chair across the counter;

shattered ceramic and glass fly through the air like shrapnel. She jerks the seat over her head and smashes it into the wall several times, with white puffs of sheetrock dust spitting forth with each blow. Pink insulation bleeds out of the hole. When her fury burns down, she heaves the bent and twisted chair out the window. The panes explode in a final punctuation of emotional turmoil.

Donna leans against the refrigerator, slides to the floor, and sits dazed for hours. Her world has imploded. As the room slowly darkens into twilight, reality seeps into her being, numbing her brain, boring into her gut. Randy may not be around for a long time to come. She lays a hand on the glass-encrusted floor to push herself upright. She doesn't feel the glass shard stick into her palm. Every muscle in her exhausted body hurts. Small plops of blood mark her progress through the kitchen, past the living room, and into their bedroom. She stops in the doorway—the double bed looks too big, too barren, too painful. She trudges like a zombie to its foot and collapses into its lonely comfort. Lying atop the covers, blood soaking into her comforter, Donna cries herself to sleep. Again.

Michael P. McLean

The Weight of the Wait

P rison waiting encompasses, and surpasses, waiting for letters, phone calls, visits, or for the parole board to release
your loved one. If you have never waited for a loved one in
prison to come home, you don't know what the "weight" of
the "wait" is like. This wait is like no other.

Living the wait is different for each person and each family
who has a loved one in prison. Mothers and fathers, sisters and
brothers, sons and daughters, wives and girlfriends, husbands
and boyfriends all cope on their own terms. Like falling in
love, or becoming a parent, some things must be experienced
to be understood.

My sweet mother, Mary, faithfully kept her heart open
for me. But she was never one to hold her tongue. She

lovingly conveyed to me how my incarceration affected not only myself but also our entire family. When your family loves you, the wait hurts them. The pain penetrates deep and strikes the heart at any time. Holidays, birthdays, the good times and bad times, all the moments that solidify a family—you're absent.

With their last breath, my mom and dad stood by me and waited for me to come home from prison. Both succumbed to lung cancer. It is the hardest weight for me to bear—the death of family and dear friends.

Who can measure the "weight" a child shoulders waiting for Daddy or Mommy to come home from prison? Kids feel and see things differently than grown-ups. When young children are in the prison visiting room, they can't understand why Mommy or Daddy won't come home with them. I can't imagine how I would feel if I had children. Not being able to raise them through their formative years or being able to contribute to the bills has consequences. While waiting for Daddy to come home, wives and grandmas have to be replacement dads. In the prison visiting room, I witness the toll that a fatherless home can have on wives and children.

⌒⌒

Wives and girlfriends often succumb to the weight of the wait. Some of them stay in their relationships with men in prison; others don't. It is one thing to be a "trooper," to stick it out for better or for worse with a man who is in prison; it's another thing for a wife to endure this ordeal with someone who doesn't appreciate her. And to wait for a man who has not changed—after decades of time behind prison walls—is to wait for him to recidivate.

Families often wait for decades for imprisoned loved ones to finally own up to their criminal ways; for some, that day never arrives. Instead, they wait for their loved ones to get out of the "box" again, or wait for them to *learn something,* after testing positive for drugs and taking the Alcohol and Substance Abuse Treatment Program again and again and again.

Waiting for God to answer prayers broadcast by people with calloused knees and wounded hearts is a ritual on both sides of the razor-wire fence.

My wife, Crystal, and I wait to hold hands behind these prison walls; we wait to eat lunch away from guards who are trained to suspect everyone of smuggling in contraband. Crystal's eyes broadcast her innermost thoughts about us, about me, about our marriage. "Michael, the wait is torture sometimes," her eyes are saying. "I'm waiting for you to come home, to see you free, and to see you be the man I know you are and can be. I don't ask or wish for much more than to cuddle up next to you on cold rainy days, and for you to snuggle beside me in our own bed. My love, I yearn to merely do everyday, mundane things with you. Having breakfast with a side order of the Sunday paper, shopping at the supermarket, and taking a long drive to nowhere are my simple plans. Honey, I'm waiting to stroll hand in hand with you through the enchanting botanical garden. I wait, wait, wait for you, for us to be the 'us' I dream of. I love, love, love you."

My wife's eyes reflect that she waits to experience the promises I have made to her, for us and our marriage. My heart reflects that, too.

I won't presume to comprehend the full weight of the wait when it comes to my wife's loneliness and emotional struggle, but I feel her pain. I'm sensitive to her tears. I know her sacrifices for me, and for us—all for love's sake. Some claim love is overrated. I say love is what matters in the end.

For a wife with a husband in prison, life is tattooed with waiting moments: waiting for the alarm to go off at 5:30 a.m., waiting for the subway or cab to take her to the Greyhound bus; then waiting for the bus, which takes her to wait to be processed into the facility, where she waits for the officer to decide if her attire is acceptable this week. Then she waits on the line to leave her husband a package, waits on the leave-funds line, waits for her man to enter the visiting room, waits on the vending machine line, waits on the microwave line. Then she waits for the intercom to spit out the announcement that visits will be terminated in fifteen minutes; she waits to savor a last kiss before she leaves; she waits to get home, where she waits to press #3 for the millionth time to accept her husband's collect call. And she waits for him to come home—not knowing if he ever will when the letters L-I-F-E are glued to the end of his sentence.

We, the incarcerated, do our own share of waiting on this side of the wall. We wait for the unit phone to ring, and for the officer to say: "On the chow!" We wait for visits, and for years to pass—one day at a time. We wait for change that never seems to come. We wait for appeals and transfers. We wait for our parole hearings. We wait for mail—some of us wait for letters that never arrive; others wait for mail delivered faithfully everyday. People wait for funds that are promised; others get only promises and not a red cent. Many of us wait to hear from friends and family who swear that they care, only to be forgotten year after year—the "out of sight, out of mind" plague knows no bounds.

Prison waiting's twin is the emotional roller coaster we ride throughout our sentences.

My time in prison has been a time of growth, and of maturity. Enlightenment has come with the price of my crime—impregnated with my own share of "waiting." But what was my wife's, or my family's crime? They are guilty only of loving and supporting me, and waiting for me to come home. I am eternally grateful, and profoundly blessed. Prison's wait has revealed to me the worst of the worst in people—they don't call it hard time for nothing. Yet, I realize that with all that I have endured, my family (my wife especially) was also sentenced to hard time. Whenever I think about this, I am overwhelmed with a piercing sense of appreciation.

I still have dreams and goals to pursue upon my release, goals that lead to the hope of a better life. Yet a top priority of mine is to shower my wife with 24–7 love. We will renew our wedding vows in Hawaii, even if I have to row her there myself! We will find ourselves in some romantic-postcard-like spot; she will be more beautiful to me than ever; and she will KNOW that the weight of the wait was worth it. I will tell her (and anyone else in earshot), "My darling wife, my God-sent wife, I am your husband and I love you. You are my best friend, and with my heart exposed, I thank you for always being in my corner, for waiting, caring, and loving me. Crystal, you will never want for love as long as my eyes are open. Your wait is over. I rededicate my love to you, to us, to our marriage."

The wait has profoundly affected both of us. I have been humbled by our love, strengthened by it, and it has been my anchor. For my wife, and all the diehard, ultra-dedicated wives who bear the weight of the wait—in the name of love, of marriage, of support—I offer this special thank you:

Dear Ones Who Wait:

You've been visiting us in the Department of Correctional Services' pinball machine for years. Your husband or significant other has ricocheted from Rikers to Clinton, then Sing Sing, zig-zagged over to Green Haven, and God only knows where to next! Like our shadows, you have followed us all this time. Perseverance is your middle name. Loyalty is tattooed across your heart. I know it's not easy for you, no matter how wide you smile at us on our visits. Your trek on that stinky sardine bus, the up-before-dawn ride, to see us; it's all got to affect you. The glazed look in your eyes reveals how sapped you've become, physically and mentally taxed from the never ending "wait," until freedom's gate opens for us.

If patience were cash, you would be a trillionaire. Instead, your bank account consists of a piggy bank on the shelf—due in part to the packages you send us more faithfully than sunshine in the summer, the bus fare expense, the collect calls you accept for what seems like the fastest thirty minutes ever! (All this you do to keep the bond solid.)

You've uttered sacred vows, "for better or for worse," but it can seem like this prison road is paved with tons of "worse." I pray that our efforts to make the "worse" moments "better" bring comfort to you. Some of us sell cards and envelopes, instead of selling drugs, to raise funds. The few dollars we have sent home every week have accumulated into a nice little emergency fund, should you need it. What a great idea to wire you some funds instead of buying that extra can of Jack Mack, or Ben and Jerry's.

A lot of us hate working in D.O.C.'s slave industry, but we love sending you Christmas and birthday presents for a change. The divine moments we are fortunate enough to share on conjugal visits pass by too quickly, we know. Watching you leave after hearing your heartbeat breaks our hearts all over again. You wonder why some of us treat you like a queen. Why? Could it be because you're the sunlight in our lives while we exist in this dungeon called prison? Your hearts know we love you, and if we weren't coming home to you one day, we would have released ourselves from your precious lives long ago. We love you too much to make you a prisoner, too—to chain you to this lifestyle for life.

We thank you for waiting, for your love, care, and life moments. Let's continue to hope, to initiate positive changes in our lives, as opposed to just "waiting" for things to happen. Keep in mind that we, too, suffer the "weight" of "waiting." Remember, focus on our future, and know that we love you.

Zee Mink-Fuller

My Son is a Number

I t was not the best news I could have heard that rainy
spring day—the doctor's unemotional voice on the phone
telling me that I was pregnant again when my firstborn was
only nine months old. It had taken me a number of years to
get pregnant the first time, so I never thought that another
pregnancy could happen so easily. My husband had recently
returned from serving in Vietnam, and we were preparing
for a life outside of the Army. There would be no insurance
to cover this birth.

We moved to the Midwest, where we had family and friends
for support. Settling into an apartment, caring for a toddler,
and adjusting to a man who seemed lost outside the regimen of
Army life was quite the chore for me. Since we had no insurance, I did not see a doctor until the time of my delivery. This

probably was not the best decision we could have made, but money was in short supply and I was a healthy young woman with no history of any physical problems. I set about making a home and preparing for another life-changing event.

My beautiful baby boy was born on a red and gold, leaf-dancing, brisk autumn day. He came into this world by way of a breech birth. My husband was not there and, as I was soon to discover, would not be around for the many trials that lay ahead. This was just the start of my son's walk along the paths of danger and fear. It was also the beginning of my lesson in unconditional love.

Soon after his birth, I discovered that my little boy was born with a kind of anemia that made him susceptible to many infections and diseases, which were always manifested in extremely high fevers. It was also at this juncture that I became a single mother, a role that I did not have time to ponder due to having two little ones demanding my full attention. Having a sick child does not give you the luxury of time to nurse a bent and battered heart.

My son's anemia was eventually cured, but eight years of raging fevers took their toll on my little son's system and his life. He fought to overcome the stigma of being a frail young boy. He had no strong, loving male influence in his life. I tried to assume both parental roles for him and his sister, but I was just not equipped to be both father and mother.

As my son grew into a teen, he became obsessed with play-ing sports, perhaps to prove to himself and everyone else that he was not this sick little kid any longer. Through hard work and determination, he achieved his athletic goals to become an award-winning athlete. He was offered scholarships, money, trophies, and even an automobile. One would think this young man had it made, with his future secure and a life of comfort waiting ahead. Yes, one would think...

Heredity's Chain

A Buster Brown blond mop circles a pale
freckled face.
Crystal blue eyes shadowed by heat of a
raging fever,
crying for hours, then quiet
with exhaustion—
Remembering those fearful days now, wishing
for those days again.
Mother knows his long-ago pain had a remedy in
a doctor's bag;
not so, for the rage in his thirty-something still
crystal blue eyes.
Confusion resides where once
greatness rented space.
Mother's unconditional love only a
Band-Aid cure for
abandoned, stunted fatherly care.

With a purchased escape, his burdens
become blessings making truth.
seen in the eye of the user, writing
the script on imaginary lines.
Liquid serum or smoking pipe put

the enemy in sheep's clothing,
wrinkles never seen.

Seeking reason is mother's quested journey,
unknotting heredity's chain,
making amends for all pain added to fever.
Twisted man, straight of heart with
a child's hope floating in
crystal blue eyes. © Zee Mink-Fuller

Years later, on one sunny autumn afternoon, my phone
rang. I thought the caller was just another reporter wanting to
interview my son, the local sports hero, for yet another story.
My son had been voted top athlete by our town's newspaper
and everyone wanted to get to know this amazing young
man. He excelled at all sports; he was a tough record-breaking
physical machine. All the teenage girls wanted a jersey with
his famous number on it. Yes, he was quite the stunning
male creature.

I answered the phone on the third ring with my usual joyful
hello. The voice on the other end was stern and male, asking
me if I was the mother of the "athlete of the year." Somehow
I knew this man was not a reporter, or a fan. I asked him who
he was and why he wanted to know about my son. In his cold
tone, he told me he was the chief of police, that I needed to
come to the police station to see my son, and that it would be
a good idea to hire an attorney. No further information was
offered, and my questions were turned away.

I nervously ran a comb through my hair, which by now had been twisted into a knot from raking my trembling fingers through it.

As I arrived at the local police station, I did not know I was about to begin a very long journey into fear and despair. I asked the girl behind the bar-covered, closed glass window about the whereabouts of my son. I had never been in a police station in my life and rarely had any contact with the police or anyone else regarding any kind of legal matter. I tried to wrap my confused mind around what the girl was telling me.

I was told to hold my driver's license up to the window, sign my name on a piece of lined paper held in place by a much-used clipboard, and sit down. I did as I was told. I slowly sat down in a dirty, hard, plastic chair alongside other people whose faces had the same stricken look that I was sure my face was wearing.

It was not long before I was led to a small room with two rows of eight chairs separated by a thick glass partition. Each chair had a small counter with a black telephone in front of it. Looking down the row of faces, I knew someone had made a mistake. My son would not be sitting anywhere with the likes of these characters.

Well, there he was, sitting in the last chair. His usually groomed blond hair was a mess and his bright blue eyes were wide with fear and desperation. Yes, someone had made a terrible mistake and that someone was my "athlete of the year" son.

It has been nearly twenty years since my virgin foray into the prison world. My son's first experience behind those cold bars was due to a night of revelry with other boys his age. That night included breaking into a residence. He learned much in his classroom cell, including how to escape—not by going over a barbed wire fence, but by using liquid escape.

The illogical decisions made by my teenage son led him down a very dangerous and criminal road. Perhaps I will never fully know why, at the peak of a budding and enviable career, he chose to enter the world of drug use and despair. I can lay blame on his having an absent father, having alcoholics for grandparents, never having enough money or, perhaps, even my own inadequacies. Whatever the reason, he is paying the lonely price of living in a world bound by iron bars—a world I get short glimpses into through the eyes of a young mother that are now on the face of an old mother who remembers praying for the fever to stop. I now pray for this caged fever to go away and bring back to me my son, who at one time only wanted to hear the word "score" on the football field, not in some dirty back alley.

My son lost all his scholarships, all his friends, most of his family, and his freedom. Yes, he lost all except for me. I still visit my son and still sit in dirty plastic chairs. My long wait should be over in another six years. My boy—yes, he is still my boy—lets me know how grateful he is for my loyalty and affirms that he could not have made it thus far without my constant love and support.

My teenage sports hero is now entering mid-life with a receding hairline, injured feet from playing too much handball to pass the time, and a body covered with prison art. The years of growing older in a confined world have made him realize the importance of family, health and, most important, freedom.

He is sad to see his mother aging from a distance. He tells me I will be forever young in his eyes, even though with each visit I know a new line has spread across my aging face.

I have waited, signed petitions, written letters to congressmen, talked with and paid huge sums of money to attorneys. I have traveled many miles, been body-searched, photographed, humiliated, and yet I wait. I listen for his phone call every Saturday, cry when we hang up, and start waiting again. I am waiting for the day when I see my son wearing jeans, a t-shirt with a football logo on the front and, most important, see his smile light up those blue eyes that have been solemn far too long. I am waiting for the day I can hug my son more than once, kiss his aging face, and sit close to him on a couch laughing at some silly television program. Waiting to see him fall in love and have a woman close to his heart. I am waiting for the day when we can sit in church together, bow our heads together, and thank God for letting my son and me raise our voices in praise together.

I wait, I answer the phone every Saturday, I pray every day, cry every night, and travel a long distance every few months to sit on hard plastic chairs, feed my son out of a vending machine, see what new artwork has appeared on his body, and cast weary eyes upon my beautiful son's face.

My son is a number. No girls are fighting to wear this number on a jersey, no reporters are calling to write about his latest record-breaking feat, and time is not being kind to the teen boy who learned how to be a man from other teen boys who also talked to their mothers through a glass partition one life-changing day long ago.

Franklin Ray Brown

Three Strikes and You're...Still In

After being in prison ten years on a twenty-five-to-life sentence for petty theft, I was asked this question by my son and daughter: "Why is the governor mad at you?"

To them it seemed an appropriate question. My son was four and my daughter was two when I came to prison. And in the ten years since then, they have seen and heard as much as any adult about what California's three strikes law is all about. Both of them are extremely bright and have asked pointed questions about why I can't come home when they need me.

When I call them and they tell me what they have been doing in school or at home and with their friends, it's wonderful to know what is going on in their lives. But it is also very painful; each time we talk, no matter what the subject matter, there is always an unspoken question looming on the outer edge of our conversations: "Daddy, I need you; when are you coming home?" Yet, out of love for me—and fear of what the answer might be—they never ask the question. But I have often thought about what my answer might be.

California's three strikes law can put people behind bars for twenty-five years to life if they commit a third felony, even if it's a nonviolent one. There have been several attempts to repeal portions of the law so that it applies only to serious and violent offenses. One of those attempts led to the most devastating day and night of my children's lives, and mine.

The attempt was in the form of an initiative on an election ballot. Before the election, polls had the initiative to repeal the law winning. For my family that meant that within ninety days after its approval, my children would have their dad home. The media fueled the perception of public support; newspapers and television stations reported that no initiative in the state's history with the kind of lead this one had in the polls had failed to pass when voted on by the electorate.

So for months prior to the election, my children and I talked about what we would do when I came home. The joy and excitement that I heard in their voices made me feel that I would be able to be a real father for the first time. We counted the days until the election.

The weekend before the election, disaster reared its ugly head. California's governor ran television ads that distorted the true intent of the initiative and who actually would be released if the measure were passed. Since these ads appeared only the weekend before the Tuesday election, they were dismissed by many as political posturing on the governor's part. Those who dismissed these last-minute ads made a huge mistake.

On election night, I called my children. I reminded them just how important a day this was in our lives. Both of them were elated. As I hung up the phone, I thought that the next time I spoke to my children would be to tell them that I would be home in a few months.

That conversation never took place.

As with all elections, returns started coming in as the polls closed. By 9:00 p.m. I was so filled with confidence and joy that I actually skipped into my cell when the day's work assignment ended. My television was programmed to scan only those channels that were reporting returns, which I planned to watch the entire night. I knew my children were watching, too. By the time they went to sleep, they saw returns that would bring their father home.

At 10:17 p.m., the numbers started to change. The initiative went from winning by twelve points to winning by only four points. At 11:30 p.m., when the numbers indicated we were winning fifty-one percent to forty-nine percent, the governor came on two of the channels I was scanning and said that they had won a great victory; he said that the initiative that would have taken me home to my children had been defeated.

I was stunned. I was angry. I was numb. I said out loud, "This cannot be happening." At 1:00 a.m., when I saw the numbers go against us by four points and remain there with almost all of the precincts having reported, I screamed. "How can this be happening?" I wailed, alone in my cell. "My God!

My God! How am I going to tell my children that I won't be coming home to them?"

I picked up my Bible and wept for God to give me strength, for at that moment I had none.

My next-door neighbor called through the vent. He asked me if I was okay. He had no television and had no idea what was happening. I stepped on my toilet to gain access to the vent, and I told him what was going on. He was silent. "This is going to destroy my children," I said. Again, he was silent. Then, through the vent, he said, "Pray. Pray for you and your children."

As I stepped down from the toilet with tears in my eyes, I saw my Bible. I placed it to my forehead and wept more. Finally, I dropped to my knees and prayed. To this day, I could not tell you what I said to God. But I do not need to remember. I had been stripped bare. All that was left to speak to God was the real me. Knowing that, I never really attempted to recall what I had prayed. That communication was pure, and should be left as such, never analyzed or repeated.

The next day was somber and tense. When we were released for our work assignments, there was a pall over everything and everyone. All around, men were speaking in whispers and shaking their heads. The officers, knowing what had occurred, respected our plight by not talking about the initiative. They knew that any improper intrusion might lead to events that they would not be able to control.

That night, when I had the opportunity to call my children, I picked up the phone and dialed their number five or six times, and each time I hung up before there was an answer. Three days passed before I could pick up the phone and complete the call.

Children are so resilient, and they sense things far beyond their years. When I finally called, they knew what had happened and what it meant to all of us. But they also sensed what it meant for me. They knew that their waiting was going to continue; they knew I was going to be in prison for a still undetermined time. They said they were sorry, and told me to be strong.

Tears streamed down my face, and I did not care who saw. My children told me that they loved me and that it was going to be okay. I could say nothing for minutes. It was only after they asked about the next time they could visit that I was able to speak.

"I just hope it's soon," I said. "I love you." They said they knew.

And, as if they knew that was all I could take, they changed the subject. My son asked me about the Eagles, who had played that weekend; he knew how much I love football and that if anything would make me feel better, that would. It did. The Eagles had won and we talked football until it was time to end the call. My daughter just blew kisses into the phone because she knew that always made me giggle. It did again.

It's been five years since that call. My children have loved me through all of those years, and I've been the best father I can be from where I am.

Now, a new opportunity, one that might take me home to my children, has presented itself. Federal judges have mandated a reduction of California's prison population because of the state's inability to adequately deliver medical treatment. As a nonviolent offender, I might be one of the 44,000-plus who may be released.

My children know about this because it's been reported in the news media. Yet, I have not spoken to them about this possibility. It's an unspoken hope that we're keeping close to our hearts. If it happens and I am blessed to go home to my family, I will cherish the opportunity it presents. If it does not happen, there will be a silent hurt. But the overt destruction of heart and hope will not be repeated.

For I know, as do my children, that waiting is hard, and another false hope of release would destroy us all.

So we wait, and I pray.

Kimberly Milberg

Waiting...

Global Tel Link. This call may be monitored or recorded. I have a prepaid call from Rachel, an inmate at .... The use of call forwarding or three-way calling is not allowed and may result in the termination of this call. Your account balance is .... If you wish to accept this call, dial.... Thank you.

This is the all-too-familiar recorded message that people hear as they wait to speak to their husbands and wives, sons and daughters, sisters and brothers, mothers and fathers, and other family and friends who are among the more than two million people incarcerated in the United States. Our country, *the* example of freedom, keeps more people locked up than any other nation in the world.

I've heard that recorded message many times as I've waited to speak to Rachel, one of those millions.

And as I sit down to write the story of waiting—for visits, bail, trial, sentencing, phone calls, classification, programs, classes, parole hearing, release—I realize that I really have three stories to tell: Rachel's story, my story, and the story of the friendship that has dramatically altered the course of both of our lives.

I am a thirty-year-old woman. I was raised in New Jersey by a single mother in a household that was less than ideal. I struggled throughout school to fit in and to find my path in the world. In high school, I was fortunate enough to volunteer in a small local hospital that quickly became my home away from home. It was a safe place, free from the violence and dysfunction of my home life. A handful of women working there took the time to let me know that they cared about me and my future. Over the many difficult years that followed after high school, I never gave up on my education or myself because I knew that those women had faith in me. Though I had one false start at college, I did graduate and eventually earned a master's degree. I am the first person in my immediate family to finish college and the only person with a master's. I attribute much of my success to knowing that there were always people rooting for me. I can never do or say enough to repay these women for all that they have done for me. However, I can *pay it forward,* and I have made it my life's work and mission to do just that.

Rachel is a twenty-one-year-old woman. She was raised in Massachusetts in a city about an hour and a half from Boston. She was also raised in a less than ideal household. When I first met her, she was fifteen and essentially homeless. She lived in foster homes and stayed out until 9:00 or 10:00 o'clock at night. She spent her time on the streets, at the soup kitchens, or wherever her mother happened to be staying at the time. She often ran away from her foster homes—but not to be on her own as many foster kids do. When Rachel ran from her foster homes, she ran back to her mother. Department of Social Services (DSS) workers would eventually find her, put her back in a foster home, and the cycle would start all over again. Eventually, DSS got sick of this, and of her. When Rachel was seventeen, DSS released her back into her mother's custody. The only problem was that her mother was in jail at the time. Rachel was officially homeless with nowhere to sleep except the streets or a shelter—neither of which was a very safe option for a seventeen-year-old girl.

One of the smartest, most resilient young women I know, Rachel made her way through the maze of social services available to her. She applied for food stamps and continued to collect the disability payments that her mother had secured for her when she was still a minor. She lived from shelter to shelter and from floor to floor (or to a couch when she was lucky). At one point, she was even working and living in an apartment with some friends.

Limited resources and the lure of street life often made illegal activities tempting and, at times, necessary for survival. When she was old enough, she started to pick up criminal charges—for theft, mostly. One night, not long after she turned eighteen, at the end of the month when money had run out, she and another young homeless woman beat up and robbed a third homeless woman for $75. They had a box cutter that they used mostly to intimidate, but also to harm their victim. The victim was hurt but would recover from her injuries. Rachel and her co-defendant were arrested shortly after the assault and Rachel's mother, who had by then been released from jail, came to find me to tell me what had happened. I had known Rachel and her mother for a number of years, having met them both while volunteering as a community organizer. Rachel's mother asked if I would visit Rachel at the county jail because, having recently been incarcerated, she could not. I agreed and, though I had known Rachel for several years, this would mark the beginning of a friendship that has changed both of our lives in ways that I don't think either of us could have ever imagined.

Waiting vs. Visiting

One of the first things I learned as I began to visit Rachel at the jail was that there were many written and unwritten rules surrounding our visits. As she was moved from prison to prison, I also learned that the rules change and that the cultures of the institutions vary. But one thing that does not change is that I always have to wait.

At the county jail where Rachel awaited trial—bail was set at $1,500, not a huge sum but well out of the reach of her family and circle of friends, who were mostly homeless and addicted—I learned that in order to be assured that I would get in to see her in the first round of visits, I had to arrive more than an hour before the scheduled visiting time. The guards would come out about a half-hour before the visit was scheduled to start and people would line up, for the most part, in the order in which they had arrived. Newer visitors were often unaware of this unwritten rule, and sometimes small arguments would break out about just who had gotten there first. Visits there were only an hour. So, more often than not, I would spend more time waiting than visiting. I saw many of the same faces waiting with me each week, and it was nice to talk with other families and friends who were also waiting to visit. Few of my friends could understand why I spent my Saturdays visiting someone who, at the time, I did not even know that well. It was nice for me to be in the company of others who, even if they didn't understand exactly why I was visiting, knew how important these visits were to the people locked up inside.

I remember my first visit with Rachel, how surprised she was to see me, and how happy she was to have a visit. Much too soon, a voice broke into the conversation that we were having on the phone through the glass that separated visitors from inmates: *Your visit is over.* That first visit ended with each of our hands pressed up against the glass; this gesture substituted for a hug. I felt compelled to return and would do so nearly every week for the next eight months.

Waiting for Bail, Trial, and Sentencing

During our weekly visits, I came to know Rachel in a way I hadn't before. I am someone who always tends to see potential over fault, and I saw in Rachel an incredibly smart young woman with endless potential and some really bad luck. I spent a lot of time thinking about how I could help her unlock her potential, much in the way that others had done for me. For her part, she could have spent her time waiting and watching the days pass by. Instead, she enrolled in classes and easily earned her G.E.D. She had been a good student growing up and now desperately wanted to go to college.

After eight months, a trial date still had not been set. On Christmas Day, I visited her and made her an offer; I would post bail for her, she would come live with me while awaiting trial, and she would start school in January. If she decided this was not what she wanted, I would continue to visit and would not make any judgment about her decision to wait for trial in the jail. Less than a week later, she came to stay in my home.

Waiting for trial was a time of many uncertainties. When would the trial be? Would the District Attorney offer her a deal? Would the victim even show up? Would she be convicted? Even with all of these unknowns, her life, and mine, had to continue. Rachel enrolled in a local community college and never missed a day except when she had to appear in court. She also reported to probation officers regularly and took other steps to get her life back in order.

Her trial began the week before spring break. By the end of the week, Rachel had been convicted. The next week, just after her nineteenth birthday, she was sentenced to three to four years in state prison, with an additional five years of probation upon her release. This was surreal. Three to four years for $75.

I knew that I would have to wait to hear from her about visits and phone calls, and I would worry until I heard that she was okay—or at least as okay as you can be if you are at the start of a three- to four-year state prison sentence.

Waiting for Phone Calls

The wait for that first phone call was interminable. Because I didn't have a landline telephone, only a cell phone, I had not been able to receive collect phone calls from Rachel when she was in the county jail. Now that she was in the state prison, I thought I would have the same problem. Luckily, she had a friend who had a landline and lived only a couple of blocks from me. We set up an elaborate system where Rachel would call her friend collect on her landline telephone, her friend would then call me on her cell phone, and I would run over to her house so that I could speak with Rachel. I didn't know the prison she was in, which made the thought of her being there immeasurably more frightening than her being in the county jail, since I had known so many people who had been there. I knew that Rachel was tough and very smart. I just hoped that she was tough enough and smart enough to figure out how to make her way in state prison. She would have to learn the rules and culture of a new institution. And so would I.

Finally, nearly a week after she had been sentenced, she called. She was okay, learning the new rules, and acclimating to the harsh realities of state prison. She had instructions for me—about visiting times and about some of the rules. Most important, when I visited, I could purchase a vending machine card so that she would be able to have some food while we visited. And, just like at the county jail, I should get to the visit early so that I could actually get in to see her.

The visits at the state prison were "contact" visits, meaning no glass separating the visitors from their friends and loved ones. This meant an extra level of sometimes ridiculous security rules and procedures. Each week, I watched the heartbreaking sight of someone getting turned away from a visit for failing to follow the detailed dress code—no jeans for women visiting women, no workout clothing (all pants had to have a zipper and button), no sandals, no camouflage prints, no jewelry, no hair bands, even though the incarcerated women are allowed to wear them, and the list went on and on.

The only good news in all the rules was that I could set up my cell phone to receive prepaid collect calls from the prison. Doing this allowed me to get calls from Rachel directly. Nearly every week in the last two years, I have waited for her call.

Waiting for Classification, Programs, Classes

I visited Rachel at the state prison for eight months. I feel fortunate that I was never turned away for a dress code infraction or rules violation. At first, I visited every two weeks; the state prison was nearly an hour and a half from where I lived. About four months into Rachel's incarceration, I moved to Boston, only about forty minutes from the prison, and resumed my weekly visits. The topic of conversation during the first months of her sentence was often the programs and classes she would be allowed to participate in. This all revolved around what she was classified to do.

Rachel worried that, because she had been convicted of a violent felony, she might be prohibited from participating in certain programs and classes. Fortunately, though it took some time, she was eventually classified to work at the prison and to take classes, which she started as soon as she was allowed. She eventually took college classes every semester through a program at Boston University. And she got one of the better-paying jobs at the prison—about $11 per week—sewing American flags. The irony of women being paid well below free-world wages to produce the symbol of the free world did not escape me. Rachel eventually became a project worker, a job that paid nearly twice as much as sewing flags and allowed her more movement around the prison. As a project worker, she was required to clean and perform simple maintenance in the prison. She also had to do snow removal at all hours of the day and night. The job was exhausting, but it kept her busy.

After about nine months, Rachel was classified to the pre-release facility across the street from the prison. Though still a prison, there are no locks on the doors and the women call the guards by their first names. There seems to be a level of mutual respect between the guards and the women not present at the main prison. Visiting is also much easier—no crazy dress code and no long waits. Most important, Rachel has been classified to work on the outside, where she has gained valuable experience and is earning a real wage. Rachel has always been a good, hard worker and she is well liked by customers and supervisors alike at the job where the prison has placed her. This has earned her a promotion and a raise. She also has been told that she will have a job when she is released from prison—no small thing for someone with a violent felony conviction. So now we wait for her release.

Waiting for Parole Hearing and Release

It is November now and there are still so many unknowns. Rachel should have a parole hearing in January or February and, if all goes well, she should be released in March. But what *should* happen isn't always what *does* happen. I don't think that Rachel or I will believe that she is being released until she walks out the door of the prison and gets into my car. Even after that, I don't know how long it will be before the reality sets in that she is home.

I try not to get too ahead of myself. I try not to picture what life will be like—hers and mine—when she is living on the outside, going to work, and to college. We have already started to make preparations. I moved to an apartment with an extra bedroom and have gotten information that she has requested about how she can continue her college education after her release. She has saved money from working and has paid back some debts.

As Rachel's release comes closer, I find myself talking about her to more people in my life. Most people, at least at first, don't understand why I have visited her all these months, and they certainly don't understand why I would choose to take her into my home. I try to explain our relationship, to give it a name. Am I a friend? A big sister? A foster parent? None of these categories really seem to entirely fit. Perhaps if I could give it a label, people would understand why Rachel and I have both chosen to share this part of our journey in life. Maybe then people could understand my commitment to her that she will always have a place to stay in my home and will always have my support. Maybe they would understand how being able to pay it forward has allowed me to feel a sense of wholeness that I had always felt was missing. They might also understand why Rachel has committed to me that she will make the best of the life that she has been given. And just like I am paying forward the kindness and support that was given to me, she will do the same for someone else when she is able.

So, as Rachel's release nears, the waiting is coming to an end. But these last months of waiting seem like some of the hardest yet. We are so close and yet so far, with so many things still unknown.

Sheila R. Rule

Seeing Joe Home

In all the years I'd loved and longed for Joe, I'd never envisioned him at home. My mind's eye had never placed him there. As I think about it now, I can only conclude that it was an unconscious act of merciful self-protection that kept me from imagining my husband in that most familiar, most comfortable, most secure and intimate place. For to envision him at home would have made my longing for him too great, too painful, nearly unbearable.

I did imagine him in other settings, in other places. On my morning walks around Washington Square Park, I often pictured him jogging ahead of me, looking back and playfully taunting me to catch up. Driving back into New York City after visiting him at the upstate prison where he is incarcerated, I sometimes saw him in the passenger seat, staring out the window in wonder at how the city had changed since he'd been gone. I envisioned him, too, at the business meetings and conferences that punctuate my life, his incisive mind always impressively on display.

But at home? Never—until Joe became a candidate for executive clemency. When it looked as if, after eighteen years in prison, his homecoming could be imminent, I unexpectedly imagined Joe smiling at me from across the kitchen table. I saw him stretched out on the living room sofa, reading the Sunday paper. I saw him asleep on his side of the bed. Never one to count on anything until it is securely in hand, I nonetheless found my mind operating as if the long wait to have Joe home could actually be over.

By any objective criteria, Joe deserved executive clemency, by which New York's governor can essentially reduce a prison sentence to time already served and grant a person's release on parole. By the force of his own will, Joe had transformed his thinking and his life, and he'd helped to change the lives of others.

He could list the array of accomplishments traditionally attained by those who use their time behind bars to turn their lives around—from model-inmate status and respected program assignments to certificates earned for strong and consistent work in voluntary therapeutic programs. But among the qualities that set him apart were his uncommon desire to draw a new roadmap for those who come from the kinds of impoverished neighborhoods he once called home—a roadmap that leads to success rather than to prison and the revolving door of recidivism—and the ways in which he has met that desire with action.

When he went to prison, Joe was a young drug dealer who had taken another man's life in a barroom scuffle. Alone in his five- by seven-foot cell, he began a long journey of deep reflection and introspection, which evolved into a journey of self-discovery. He found guidance in church sermons, he read books that allowed him to explore his African-American identity, and he followed those with self-help and motivational books. To shore up his innate business skills and feed his interest in entrepreneurship, he read everything he could get his hands on related to personal finance and business. He even traded cigarettes for books in order to build his own business library. Word spread among fellow incarcerated men that he could help them with personal finance issues and business-related questions, and he soon became the authoritative advisor to men seeking guidance on such matters.

In 1995, he began formally teaching personal finance classes. Working with his eager students, he realized how engaged people were with what he had to say and that he had something to contribute to society's welfare. He realized that he had a way to honor his potential, and the potential of the young man whose life he took in that barroom fight. By the time he was chosen for the clemency process, he had taught hundreds of men in the various facilities in which he'd lived. Those classes led him to develop Inmates Teaching Entrepreneurship and Mentoring (ITEM). Founded with Steve Mariotti, a mentor of Joe's who is a former Wall Street executive and president of the internationally recognized Network for Teaching Entrepreneurship, ITEM trains the incarcerated to teach their children and others who are in prison the basics of business ownership.

As Joe embraced his passion for teaching, he began to feel that his life had meaning. I entered his life in 2002, through my volunteer work with the prison ministry at Riverside Church, and we were married in 2005 in a prison visiting room. Joe and I would often talk about how we wanted to help our people, how we wanted to "give back." In that spirit, he decided to write a book intended to encourage people currently or formerly in prison to use what for many are innate entrepreneurial gifts to build better lives and break the brutally predictable cycle of recidivism. The result of his efforts was a well-respected and nationally distributed book, *Think Outside the Cell: An Entrepreneur's Guide for the Incarcerated and Formerly Incarcerated,* which Joe sees as a first step in eventually providing entrepreneurial education, mentoring, and start-up capital to this population across the country. If the letters and e-mails we have received are any indication, the book has offered hope to and helped to redirect the thinking of hundreds of men and women across the nation who have prison in their backgrounds.

For society at large, Joe began drawing a new roadmap, too, one that takes views and attitudes about the incarcerated and formerly incarcerated in new directions. Among the research papers he'd written was one examining the way New York State's Department of Correctional Services and Division of Parole determine the level of risk an incarcerated person, if released, would pose to public safety. The report concludes that "high risk"—as it relates to crime and public safety—must be redefined so that the emphasis is not solely on the nature of an offender's crime, which can never be changed, but also on whether the offender is now likely to commit another crime.

We put all of these details, as well as our hearts, into Joe's clemency application. I mailed the application to the governor's office in September 2008, along with copies of all the letters from prominent citizens who were calling for Joe's release. When Joe wasn't one of the two people granted clemency that December, the month the decisions are traditionally announced, we were disappointed. But since Joe hadn't received a formal denial, we held out hope.

On a chilly November evening nearly a year later, I was walking home from a book party when I checked my cell phone for messages. There were two rather frantic ones from my close friend Rose, both alerting me that Joe had called her looking for me, that he was desperately trying to reach me. Feeling a rush of anxiety, I quickened my pace and called Rose back. She told me that she didn't know why Joe needed to speak to me; he just did. I immediately thought the worst. But as my apartment building came into view, this thought suddenly came to me: Maybe there's good news about clemency.

I held that thought as I waited for Joe's call, but high anxiety elbowed it out of the way when the telephone finally rang. At the end of the familiar recording announcing that I had a call from a correctional facility, I stepped on Joe's familiar greeting of "Hey, Sugah," with a desperate, "What's wrong?!"

Joe told me what he'd told Rose, before vowing her to secrecy: He'd been informed by the parole officer at his prison that he was a candidate for clemency. From hundreds of applicants requesting clemency, he had been selected to go through the process.

I couldn't contain my joy. I cried. I screamed. I hooped and hollered. I thanked God, over and over and over again.

We were now so close. We were almost there. Joe was almost home. And when I awoke the next morning, I could clearly imagine him asleep next to me in bed.

Joe was almost immediately moved to another prison, where the clemency hearing would take place. He was joined by nine other men from prisons around the state who had been selected for the process; there were also two women, who went through the proceedings at a women's facility. The day before his hearing, I visited him. We held hands, hugged, talked about what questions might be asked. He seemed calm; I tried to be.

The next day, Joe and the others appeared one by one before commissioners of the state parole board, who would then make a recommendation about release to the governor. I could feel my heart pounding that entire day. When Joe called me later that day, he said that he thought the hearing had gone well. He'd spoken his truths and said everything he wanted to say. He said that he and the other men who were up for clemency had given each other encouragement. Some of their stories were particularly compelling; surely someone among them would be going home. That evening, as I donned a fancy dress to attend the National Book Awards ceremony and dinner, one of the most important events on the nation's literary calendar, I imagined Joe looking incredibly handsome in a tux.

Five days later, a parole officer visited my apartment to do the requisite home study that families undergo before a loved one is released on parole. She took a look around, complimented me on my home, and talked about the guidelines to which Joe would need to adhere. She talked as if Joe's release was a sure bet. After she left, my emotions swung back and forth. One moment I was pushing myself toward my natural inclination to not count my chickens before they hatched, and the next moment I was excitedly making plans for Joe's homecoming.

That emotional back-and-forth was my constant shadow in the month and a half until we got the clemency decision. So, too, were high anxiety and unyielding stress. I sometimes caught myself literally holding my breath. I jumped when the phone rang. I read tea leaves. I scanned the daily paper for any signs about how the governor's political plans might affect his clemency decisions; my heart took a nosedive over front-page news about the murder of four police officers in Washington State at the hands of a man who'd been granted clemency years earlier by Mike Huckabee, when he was governor of Arkansas. I asked friends and family for Bible verses that could quell the stress, the tension, the anxiety, the intensity of it all. I started carrying a pocket-size Bible and I would whip it out and read the recommended verses whenever my feelings threatened to overwhelm me. My morning prayers seesawed from pleadings to send Joe home to words of gratitude that Joe was coming home. My life was totally consumed with thoughts of Joe and clemency and his coming home. And images of Joe at home became a fixture in my imagination.

Joe was consumed with thoughts of home, too. He felt as if he could actually be on the threshold of a new life, a new beginning. He felt as if prison might soon be a hard memory. But because he is calmer and more emotionally centered than I under any circumstances, he would meet my anxiety with a quiet confidence that he'd done his best, and a quiet hope that his best was good enough. Word was out around the prison that he was a candidate for clemency, and it seemed that someone was always coming up to him and asking, "Have you heard yet? Have they told you when you're going home?" The general expectation, among incarcerated men and correctional officers alike, was that all of Joe's personal qualities and accomplishments would lead to a favorable clemency decision. While Joe wasn't as sure as they were, he sent home some of his shirts and sweaters and most of his beloved books, in the hope that he'd soon follow them.

The decision came three days after Christmas. All of the years of transformation, all of the hard work and anticipation, all of the anxiety and prayers seemed to boil down to a standard form letter that was carelessly misdated December 24, 2006—the year was 2009—and that read in part, "After a careful review of this case, it has been determined that there is insufficient basis to warrant the exercise of the Governor's clemency powers." We would learn later that all of the good men and women who were candidates for clemency with Joe were denied.

When he called me with the news, Joe's main concern was how I'd take it. He wanted to make sure that I was okay. I was stunned, unbelievably saddened, emotionally bloodied. I felt like I was falling backwards through space. But with the necessary time to heal, I trusted that I'd eventually be okay. So I assured him that I was. I wanted to know that he was okay, too. Yes, he told me. And then, as I tried to settle in what I assumed to be our mutual grief, Joe yanked me into a full-throttle conversation about all of the work we needed to do to bring about parole reform, along with the steps that he and other men at his facility were undertaking to complement the parole reform work of the criminal justice policy group to which I belong.

Such is Joe's way. Although he is introspective and reflective, he does not spend much time engulfed in his emotions. With his extraordinary willpower, he gets on with things. He charges ahead. He makes plans. He gets things done. I, on the other hand, find that allowing myself to fully experience my emotions—to even wallow in them for a respectable period of time—is part of my healing process. I think it's healthy, the way to wholeness and full recovery.

I felt that, like me, Joe needed to find some way to allow himself to fully experience his emotions in order to fully recover. For even though he had not driven himself crazy as I had during the clemency process, his yearning to be free runs deep, and to see the door shut so hard on his dreams of home had to be traumatic. Joe needed to take time to heal, to tend to his battered heart and battered hope. He needed to acknowledge the hurt, the sadness, the pain. As I allowed my feelings to envelop me—and as I found solace in unquantifiable portions of fried and greasy comfort food—I told Joe that he needed to let his feelings have their say.

But behind prison walls, it's hard—and sometimes dangerous—to relax the shoulders, to give in to feelings, to allow sadness to simply be. So, Joe tried to keep his emotions in check. With friends on the inside, he talked matter-of-factly about what had happened, how he'd been denied. There were no tears, no visible sadness; he even managed a smile now and then. He carried on with prison's daily grind; he had no choice. Yet, in our telephone conversations, he became unusually quiet, distant. He seemed tired, listless. He seemed unfocused. My "get-on-with-things" Joe appeared to be standing still. Where he always sought to guide me, prod me, lecture me, and encourage me as I carried out the work of the publishing company I founded several years ago, he now had little to contribute.

In February, we had a two-day conjugal visit; it's called a "trailer," for the homey trailers on prison grounds where those visits take place. Our trailers had always included big dreams about our future, the steps we needed to take to make one project or another a reality, the steps we needed to take to bring Joe home. This trailer was devoid of such talk. In fact, it was devoid of much talk at all. So much so that I eventually turned to Joe and said, "I miss you."

Months later, Joe was able to put words to his feelings in this part of a letter to me:

When I received the form letter from the clemency bureau informing me that my clemency application had been denied, I was rendered numb. Breathless. Confused. Saddened. Angry.

I knew I deserved it, and you and I had pulled out all the stops—preparing a first-class clemency package, getting letters of support from respected people across the country, etc.—in order to bring about my release.

For the next couple of months everything seemed weird, otherworldly. C.O.s greeted me with "I heard you're going home soon. Good for you." I had to tell them that my application had been denied. That I'd reapply in a year. Not a day went by that I didn't have to repeat this fact to someone. It seemed like all eyes were on me. It was painful. I'd come so close to being released, so close to reuniting with my son, so close to making a life with you in real time. I'd come so close to being able to realize my full potential, so close to being able to fully honor the potential of the young man whose life I took.

Everything annoyed me: Waiting in line to get on one of the two phones in my housing unit. Frivolous conversations and gossip. Feigned sympathy. The food served tasted worse by the day. I'd eat a few spoonfuls and then resort to gorging on junk food, even late at night. I must've gained ten pounds in three months.

I'd make excuses for not going outdoors to work out: "It looks like it's going to rain." "It's too cold outside." "I have important 'stuff' to work on, to tend to."

I felt myself slipping, becoming unglued. Becoming detached from everyone—you, my family, my friends, myself. I simply needed time to myself. I had no idea how much time I needed, *but I needed it. But that was a luxury I didn't have. If only I could be transplanted to a tropical island, I thought, where I could be left alone.*

Although I was always happy to see you when you came to visit me, even our visits felt different. They brought more sadness than joy. They reminded me that even though we'd been through a lot over the previous months, even though we'd experienced a new and different chapter in our lives, at the end of the day nothing had changed. We were still subjected to the prying stares of C.O.s. We were still subjected to insane package rules. And I was still subjected to strip frisks at the end of our visits. I'd return from our visits feeling emotionally depleted—but grateful for having you in my corner, in my life.

Throughout this time, I kept my game face on. I tried not to let on how much pain I had swirling inside, how much sadness. I continued to teach classes here and there, including a clemency class. But I was gradually becoming withdrawn from most things prison-related. I focused on parole matters, working with the group of men who also dedicated their time to studying parole. I had little interest in anything else.

Although it was unlike me, I even lost interest in the projects you worked on on behalf of the incarcerated, the formerly incarcerated and their loved ones. I just wanted to go home.

Then came our trailer visit. Usually, I'm excited about spending two days alone with you. Usually I'm full of energy, full of ideas. This time, as you know, I had no energy, no ideas. It was on that trailer that I finally took your advice and let go. I allowed myself to feel the full weight of depression. I crashed.

You tried to reach me, to comfort me. But it was too late. Even if I had wanted to hold in the flood of emotions, I could not.

While I didn't shed tears, by simply allowing myself to sit with my anger, my sadness, my depression, I experienced an emotional cleansing like I'd never felt. I rid myself of the bottled-up toxins and replenished my spirit with my trademark hope and optimism. I refueled on God's grace and mercy. I basked in your love and support.

Next time, I told myself after that trailer. Next time, I will be granted clemency.

After that trailer, Joe became Joe again. He got on with things. He charged ahead. He made plans. He developed sample legislation for parole reform. He was instrumental in developing the Prison to Prosperity Fair, a holistic reintegration fair for New York City's formerly incarcerated. He and two fellow incarcerated men—Bruce Bryant and William Holmes—created the first prisoner gun buy-back program in New York State, and the three were joined by Stanley Bellamy, who's also incarcerated, to form the Civic Duty Initiative Group. The men aim to help combat social ills in poor communities—social ills that led to their incarceration in the first place. And on top of all that, Joe gave me ideas and more ideas for my business, for my various projects.

I got on with things, too. But I can't stop envisioning Joe at home. My mind's eye won't let me. And sometimes the longing is too great, too painful, nearly unbearable.

CONTRIBUTORS

In addition to offering biographical information, the authors express their hopes and dreams for themselves and humanity, as well as gratitude to the special people in their lives.

Franklin Ray Brown

I'm from Fresno, California, and I've been writing since 1980. My major accomplishments are Tomeia, Kashayla, Alay'e, and Kiara—my children. Then there's "Felonise," without whom I would have never known what real love and commitment were about. May my grandmother, mother, and Doug Nelson, another family member, rest in peace. I lost them while waiting for California's three strikes law to be amended so that it is what it was intended to be, not what it was perverted to be.

Jennifer Collins

I live in Hicksville, on Long Island, with my loving and supportive husband, Michael, and my beautiful son, Michael

Joseph, who's now a toddler. I have been writing poetry and short stories since I was thirteen years old. Writing for me is an instrument to help navigate and understand the world and my experiences. It is my compass, guiding me through the rough and quiet waters of my life. I am also a licensed social worker and a certified yoga instructor. Like writing, yoga has sustained me and helped me cope during difficult times. They have also helped me to keep it "real." I'd love to develop a writing and yoga program that helps people connect with their authentic voices and wisdom.

Jason Dansby

I am a native North Carolinian—from Asheville, to be exact. My greatest accomplishments are my children. My main goal is that after I have been called to the Lord, my children look back over my life and view me as a success. I have three biological children—Dejaun, five; Ricardo, three; and Zacharie, two—and three stepchildren. I hope the future brings them the same great opportunities I have been blessed with. The fact that our president is half-black and half-white has shown my children and me that there are no more excuses for not doing something with our lives. My greatest hope for my future is to be looked at as a person who, despite having done wrong, has decided to rise above the proverbial shackles linking me to a past of nothingness. I would like the readers of *The Think Outside the Cell Series* to read my stories and know that just because you have hit rock bottom doesn't mean you cannot dust yourself off and climb to the top. Some people might prejudge you, but the most important people will judge you by the content of your character, not by the content of your rap sheet.

Ebonny Fowler

I am a personal trainer, fitness instructor, mentor, and advocate in New York City. I enjoy staying active in my community and helping others maintain a healthy lifestyle. As a volunteer with SAVI—the Sexual Assault and Violence Intervention program—I assist rape victims and survivors of domestic violence in hospital emergency rooms. I'm also a mentor with the Big Brothers Big Sisters program. I received a bachelor's degree from Johnson C. Smith University, where I studied television and radio broadcasting and journalism. My work has appeared in several publications, including *Essence, XXL* and *The Source*. I've also hosted and produced two of my own entertainment television shows, *Ebonny Eyes* and *EB ON NY*.

Delores Mariano

I was born in Los Angeles—yes, a real Californian. My ethnic heritage is rich, with roots in Prussia, Sicily, Germany, and, eight centuries back, Ethiopia. I have two daughters and a beautiful granddaughter, who is a toddler and a handful. My son died in 2008. My mother is in her late eighties and full of life. I've had medical problems and was pronounced dead twice in prison and once on the outside. I beat death so that I could make a positive difference for women who are beaten down inside prison walls. My passion is to find release and relief for women who are falsely imprisoned or imprisoned past their real release dates. I want to give them hope that they will have a tomorrow. Much love to all, and respect to those who will print the truth.

Michael P. McLean

I'm in my mid-forties, and I firmly believe that the best years of my life are ahead of me. Coming to prison was a turning point in my life. From that rock-bottom experience has come my growth, my metamorphosis, a state of decency. I'm fascinated by outer space, nature, magic, human potential—life! I love laughter and simple conversation with my beloved wife, Crystal; making her smile is a source of joy for me. Writing allows me to express myself and my ideas while touching others. After my parents, Ivon and Mary, died of lung cancer caused by smoking, I became a certified tobacco cessation specialist. My calling is to help people quit that deadly habit. I hope to become the top tobacco cessation specialist in the world!

Ninowtzka Mier

I'm an attorney at a South Florida law firm, where I specialize in insurance defense and tort law. I also work *pro bono* on immigration cases. I recently successfully defended a single mother who was threatened with deportation to Jamaica. She and her son may now seek permanent residency and eventually U.S. citizenship. I am passionate about developing alternatives to mandatory minimum sentences for nonviolent offenders. A daughter of Colombian parents, I was born and raised in South Florida. I am a contributing writer for *Sue Magazine* and the Organization of Legal Professionals. I enjoy competing in triathlons, and I love playing with my dog, Lola, a sweet Lab I adopted from the Humane Society. I refer to her as my "society girl."

Kimberly Milberg

I'm originally from Lawrenceville, New Jersey. In high school, I was fortunate to volunteer at a local hospital that became a home away from home. I met women there who, because of their unconditional positive support, would have an immeasurable impact on my life. It is for these women that I committed my life to paying it forward. I moved to western Massachusetts in 1996 to attend the University of Massachusetts, Amherst. After a number of years in human service work, I returned to school and in 2005 earned a master's degree from the Smith College School for Social Work. I also participated in a number of grassroots activist campaigns—including in a local Critical Resistance chapter and the Statewide Harm Reduction Coalition—and worked to expand needle-exchange programs and to stop new prison and jail construction. In 2007, I moved to Boston, where I am a social worker, and training for my first marathon.

Zee Mink-Fuller

I am an antiques dealer and appraiser, mother and grand-mother, with an unstoppable desire to write. After years of being a "closet" writer, I am now, at the young age of sixty-one, sending my words out to the world of rejection letters. I share my life experiences with others in the hope that my words can somehow soothe their aching hearts. I live on a small quiet farm close to a large metropolitan city, which gives me an ample supply of subjects to constantly stoke my imagination. My dream is to make a difference one word at a time, through the grace of God. With my daughter, a young breast cancer survivor, I have started a nonprofit foundation called Pink Outlaw in order to help cancer victims.

Lowanna M. Owens

I live in Diamond Bar, California, with my husband of thirty-two years and two of our three adult children. I wrote my essay because of my passion to help our young black men find hope despite the mental and societal bondage that keeps them from shining. My other passions include excellence, reading, writing, collecting postage stamps and other items, the R&B groups the Whispers and the Impressions and, since the early 70s, recycling. For my life, these are the rules: 1) God is first; 2) family always; 3) friends forever; 4) fun and laughter often; 5) prayer daily for forgiveness, salvation, gratitude, healing, and for others; 6) abuse of no one or no thing; 7) reality is the only truth and should not be mixed up with negativity; 8) good character, manners, and style matter; 9) communication and action should match; 10) listen and learn; 11) recognize faults; 12) sorrow and problems are unavoidable—joy and coping are obtainable; 13) laughing, as appropriate, heals; 14) prayer works; 15) I may not be able to forget, but will forgive and keep the faith; 16) be on time; 17) always unexpectedly do something for or say something nice to another person.

Randy Peters

I loved writing in high school but because of financial problems had to give it up and go to work. A little over twenty years later, I had the chance to pick it up again and have been running with it ever since. I've been writing seriously for about two and a half years now. I've had several pieces published locally and completed a novel about a wolf pack pushed out of its home and forced to flee after killing a farmer. I am currently working on a novel about a northern Vermont boy growing up amidst alcoholism and abuse. I continue to write short stories and poetry, hoping for placement in ever-larger publications. My wife, Donna, is my largest source of support. She has always been there for me, through good times and bad. I owe all my success to her unwavering love and devotion. The Community High School of Vermont has helped me with technical aspects of my writing, reference books, and computer access.

Sheila R. Rule

I am founder and president of Resilience Multimedia, a publishing company that reflects my passion for social justice. My first contribution was a self-help book called *Think Outside the Cell: An Entrepreneur's Guide for the Incarcerated and Formerly Incarcerated,* by Joseph Robinson, my husband. I received a grant from the Ford Foundation to produce my next project, a series of books—including this one—designed to present a fairer, more balanced image of the incarcerated, the formerly incarcerated, and their loved ones. Before becoming a publisher, I was a journalist at *The New York Times* for more than thirty years. My beats included the New York State Legislature, social services, the homeless, civil rights, and pop music. I was also a foreign correspondent in Africa and Europe. I was a senior editor when I retired from *The Times* in order to fully embrace publishing. Joe and I have a striving, working marriage and two sons, Sean and Joseph.

Lawrence J. Schulenberg

I am a polio survivor, a loving husband, an adoptive father, a retired high school teacher and principal, and an adjunct instructor at the community college in Council Bluffs, Iowa. I graduated from Northwest Missouri State University, and also hold degrees from Central Missouri State and Creighton University. When post-polio syndrome forced me to retire as a principal, my college sweetheart and wife, Pat, strongly urged me to find an activity so that I could keep busy and not be underfoot. So I dusted off a murder mystery that I had begun years earlier; I only wanted one book with my name on the cover. I've now got four books on the shelf: *Dead at the Desk, To Catch the Snowflakes, Willie McGuire and the Land of the People,* and *Dead and Dixie Fried.* I continue to be very interested in prison sentencing reform, and I contact my legislators to work on behalf of the many incarcerated men and women in our country. Through my membership on the State of Iowa Fourth Judicial District Department of Corrections Board of Directors, I work to improve the situation. I'll probably never retire from teaching. I do believe that when I was born, God pointed down from heaven and said, "This one will be a teacher."

Jeff Smith

I'm a freelance translator in Cincinnati, having moved to the city forty years ago for graduate school. I previously taught German at the college level for five years and worked as a product manager for a German firm. I am still struggling to reinvent myself after the loss of my son. My wife, Diane Debevec, and a small and unselfishly giving network of close friends provide invaluable love and support.

Whitney Holwadel Smith

Whitney Holwadel Smith was born in Cincinnati on April 10, 1984, and died at United States Penitentiary Terre Haute in Indiana on April 4, 2009. He and his sister grew up in an upper-middle-class family, surrounded by loving and caring grandparents, aunts, and uncles. His early life would be considered privileged yet unremarkable by those standards: family camping trips and vacations in Costa Rica and Europe, beloved pets, good schools, and the divorce of his parents when Whit was thirteen. Drug abuse and disciplinary issues in school, along with an impulsive side that he seemed often unable to control, even as he felt genuine remorse afterward, eventually led to the robbery of a store when he was seventeen, for which he received three years in an Ohio state adult prison. Five months after returning home, he was convicted of unarmed bank robbery and sentenced to six years at the maximum-security Federal prison in Terre Haute. With just over half that sentence completed, Whit apparently committed suicide. Whit had always been a truly gifted writer, and during the last six months of his life he wrote a personal blog that found enthusiastic and compassionate readers all over the world. Whit's blog can still be read at *http://whit-superfriends. blogspot.com.*

Ashley White

I was born and raised in Rochester, New York. When I met my husband, it was instant love. He made me realize that true love does exist. The prison system cannot stop the love we have for each other. I had many hopes for us and the future, and even though they are now on hold, we plan to accomplish them upon his release. Two of my goals are to return to school and travel. I have one son. He's nine years old and a wonderful young man. It's because of him and my husband that I have the strength and power to make it through the day. I want everyone to know that just because someone is incarcerated, that doesn't mean that he or she belongs there. There are innocent people in prison, too. I love you, Brad!

Editors' Bios

Sheila R. Rule is founder of Resilience Multimedia, a publishing company that seeks to present a fairer image of the incarcerated, the formerly incarcerated, and their loved ones. A journalist at *The New York Times* for more than thirty years before retiring from that newspaper, she was led to publishing by her love of books and her respect for the power of stories.

Marsha R. Rule (Marsha R. Leslie) is a writer and editor for UW Medicine, University of Washington, Seattle. She edited *The Single Mother's Companion: Essays and Stories by Women* (Seal Press, 1994) and contributed to *The Black Womens' Health Book* (Seal Press, 1990, 1994). She lives in Seattle.

Order Form

Ordering Method:

Telephone: Call 877-267-2303 toll free.
Have your credit card ready.

Email: *resiliencemultimedia@verizon.net*

Postal: Resilience Multimedia, Dept. B,
511 Avenue of the Americas, Suite 525
New York, NY 10011

Online: *www.thinkoutsidethecell.org*

All books are $14.95 plus shipping:
$3.50 (book rate; delivery speed varies)
$5.75 (priority mail; approx. 1–3 days)

New York residents, please add 8.875% sales tax.
Discount schedule for bulk orders is available upon request.

Number of Copies Requested:

_____ *Love Lives Here, Too: Real-Life Stories about Prison Marriages and Relationships*

_____ *Counting the Years: Real-Life Stories about Waiting for Loved Ones to Return Home from Prison*

_____ *The Hard Journey Home: Real-Life Stories about Reentering Society after Incarceration*

_____ *Think Outside the Cell: An Entrepreneur's Guide for the Incarcerated and Formerly Incarcerated*

Name:_____

Address:_____

City: _____State:_____Zip: _____

Daytime phone: _____

Email address: _____

Payment: ❑ Check payable to Resilience Multimedia

❑ Credit card: ❑ Visa ❑ MasterCard ❑ Amex ❑ Discover

Card number: _____ Exp. Date:_____

Name on card:_____